# the adventure
# of fasting

# the adventure of fasting

**A PRACTICAL GUIDE**

## James Lee Beall

Fleming H. Revell Company
Old Tappan, New Jersey

Unless otherwise identified, all Scripture quotations are from the King James Version of the Bible.

Scripture references identified RSV are from the Revised Standard Version of the Bible, copyrighted 1946 and 1952.

Scripture references identified AMPLIFIED are from AMPLIFIED BIBLE, Old Testament. Copyright © 1962,64 by Zondervan Publishing House and are used by permission.

Library of Congress Cataloging in Publication Data

Beall, James Lee.
    The adventure of fasting.

    Bibliography: p.
    1. Fasting.  I.  Title.
BV055.B4    248'.273    74–10741
ISBN 0–8007–0683–8

*To*
*my daughter, Analee,*
*a father's delight*

# Contents

# Preface

## Does Fasting Really Work?

This is a day of pragmatic values. Things are measured by whether or not they produce their intended results. This is true in the world of business and science; it is also true in the church. We are looking for the mechanics of success, and for shortcuts to conserve time, energy, and finances.

Fasting is one of those practices that is periodically suggested as a shortcut in obtaining answers to prayer. Every so often it spreads across the nation as a fad, and many testify to receiving new power with God.

Fasting is sometimes advertised almost as a gimmick or cure-all. It is supposed to be effective in procuring power in prayer, in obtaining divine protection, in granting clearer revelation, in giving deliverance from the demonic and from sickness, and even as producing a purer spiritual life.

On the other hand, fasting has been ignored by the large majority of Christians except as a prescribed duty in connection with special days. The church as a whole has yet to recover from the extreme legalism and even asceticism of the early and medieval church. Some people are beginning to recognize the need for a restoration of balance in understanding the function of fasting.

William Kelly urges the establishment of the intended purposes of fasting. He writes in *Baker's Dictionary of Theology:*

. . . Christian history gives ample evidence of the abuse as well as the
proper use of fasting. From an early period legalism invaded this
biblical and intrinsically valuable practice, special days and periods
being imposed and distinctions made between what might or what
might not be eaten. In reaction against this perversion, the evangelical churches have been tempted to remedy the abuse by discontinu-
ing the practice altogether rather than restoring it to its proper use
in individual and congregational life. Yet fasting is obviously a biblical
practice capable of a profitable use. In face of corruption, the true
aim should be to restore it to its evangelical setting and purpose.

Two recent books reflect this trend to reestablish fasting in
right perspective. Both are very well written and highly infor-
mative. Arthur Wallis has written an entire book examining
every aspect of scriptural fasting. Appropriately it is titled
*God's Chosen Fast.* Derek Prince has developed the theme of
prayer and fasting as intercession for national needs. In this
treatise, Prince urges the application of biblical principles to
bring about God's promised results. The title is *Shaping History through Prayer and Fasting.*

Why, then, are we writing yet another book on the subject
of fasting?

It is my contention that in this day of charismatic renewal,
God is restoring to the church the original simple meanings of
many truths. Not only are the basic foundations of salvation
being restored to their spiritual significance, but the practical
aspects of Christian living are once again being restored to
biblical meaning. Fasting (along with prayer, almsgiving, tith-

ing, footwashing, and other practical aids to life in Christ) is
due for a fresh understanding.

## First the Natural

There is a principle for illustrating truth found all through
Scripture: the natural pictures the spiritual. In fact, most of the
Old Covenant consisted of types and shadows—that is,
picture-stories—to portray better things to come which would
be spiritual. The writer of the Hebrews Epistle refers to these
lessons as "figures of the true."

The Apostle Paul makes use of this principle in explaining
the doctrine of resurrection from the dead. This is a concept
beyond our imagination; we need a natural illustration. So Paul
tells us that the person we will be after death has been pre-
viewed in what we have been in this life. Paul uses what we
already know as a basis for comparison.

> And so it is written, The first Adam was made a living
> soul; the last Adam was made a quickening spirit. How-
> beit that was not first which is spiritual. . . . The first
> man is of the earth, earthy: the second man is the Lord
> from heaven. . . . And as we have borne the image of
> the earthy, we shall also bear the image of the heavenly.
>
> 1 Corinthians 15:45-47, 49

Taking this biblical form for illustrating truth, I propose that
fasting speaks of far more than abstaining from food and the
obvious physical results. Rather, the outward actions speak of
an inner focus upon God, an intensity of turning from all else,
and a complete readjusting of priorities. Fasting is provided to

help us maintain or restore balance and perspective in Kingdom living.

## An Invisible Kingdom

The Kingdom of God cannot be seen by the natural eye. It requires a spiritual entrance into the realm where Jesus Christ reigns. This entrance is called in Bible terms "being born again." It involves a total conversion of the inner man and the impartation of the life of God through the Holy Spirit.

This truth of a spiritual realm where God rules and His will truly is accomplished was difficult even for a teacher of the Jews to understand. For example, Nicodemus kept interpreting spiritual truths according to their natural counterparts. He could not make the transition from the natural to the spiritual. Jesus told Nicodemus:

> . . . Except a man be born again, he cannot see the kingdom of God. . . . except a man be born of water and of the Spirit, he cannot enter into the kingdom of God. That which is born of the flesh is flesh; and that which is born of the Spirit is spirit.
>
> John 3:3, 5, 6

These words sound so simple, even nursery level. But Nicodemus did not understand them. Instead he visualized a repeat of natural birth. He missed the whole idea of a spiritual kingdom. Jesus was surprised.

> . . . Art thou a master in Israel, and knowest not these things? Verily, verily, I say unto thee, We speak that [which] we do know, and testify that [which] we have

seen; and ye receive not our witness. If I have told you
earthly things, and ye believe not, how shall ye believe,
if I tell you of heavenly things?

John 3:10-12

This is a common problem in religion: forms which are
meant to communicate spiritual truth are seen instead as ends
in themselves. They lose their power to function as language
because the connection between the natural symbol and its
corresponding reality is lost. Only the Holy Spirit can enable
us to perceive what God is doing through such natural elements as the water of baptism, the bread and wine of the
Lord's Supper, and the absence of food in fasting.

Fasting is a means of reminding ourselves that the Kingdom
is more than we perceive with our senses. It is a call to look
beyond the illustration and to allow the Holy Spirit to make the
Kingdom of God so real that it occupies first place in our
aspirations. Fasting enables us to make the transition from
natural to spiritual perspective. It is a deliberate choice to set
aside the temporal in pursuit of the spiritual.

For the kingdom of God is not meat and drink; but
righteousness, and peace, and joy in the Holy Ghost.

Romans 14:17

Let us examine this discipline in detail and discover whether
or not fasting performs within us God's intended purposes.
Does it transfer our focus from ourselves and earthly concerns
to God? Does it free us from our self-preoccupation to involve
ourselves in the needs of others? Is there a valid spiritual reason
for physical fasting?

# the adventure
# of fasting

# 1

# Fast? What For?

"Why would the Lord want us to fast? What could this possibly accomplish for us? Surely God isn't interested in our dining habits; God is too big for that!"

These are some of the questions which formed in my mind while I was yet a boy. During my teen years, I remember ministers who visited our church who referred to days of fasting. Again I would wonder why. "Why did that man fast?"

It wasn't until after World War II ended that I heard anything more of fasting. About 1948, new interest in physical healing became evident all over the country and with it the matter of fasting. At that time fasting was being taught as a means to gain power with God to heal the sick and to deal with enemy oppression. Some of the books published on fasting at that time were of the sensational type. They presented fasting as a "spiritual cure-all" for nearly everything. Others advocated "spiritual atomic energy" if a person fasted the Prophet's Fast of forty days in length. These books repelled me. Fasting simply did not make sense. I dropped the matter.

Periodically, the question of fasting would surface again. In fact, whenever and wherever the spiritually hungry would gather, questions would inevitably be raised about fasting. But again, I heard little that was conclusive or convincing.

A resurgence of interest in fasting has accompanied today's charismatic renewal. The whole issue of fasting is being reexamined. Perhaps there is something to it! It is rare for me to conduct any series of meetings and not be confronted with questions related to fasting.

## Facing the Issue

Up until recently, I had a "pat answer" to all the questions on fasting. I would refer my inquirers to the episode involving Jesus and the Pharisees. The Pharisees asked Jesus why His disciples did not fast in the manner of those who followed John the Baptist. Jesus told them His disciples had no need to fast so long as He, the Bridegroom, was with them. When it was time for His departure to heaven, it would in turn be the time for His disciples to fast.

My understanding of this scriptural passage at that time was, "The Lord is with me and while I am aware of His presence, fasting is not necessary for me." Consequently, I rarely fasted.

But, instinctively, I knew this was not the way of integrity. My "pat answer" did not cover the entire scriptural picture of fasting. There were gaps and I knew it.

I forced my way into the Bible with some relish, but admittedly still with my subsurface reservations—fasting was not really to my liking; it was bound to alter my way of living.

My struggle with the idea of fasting did not necessarily stem from my wanting food—I have never been a heavy eater—but it meant inconvenience and I like an orderly, arranged world. With some trepidation, I pushed ahead.

I found that fasting was first mentioned in the New Testament by Jesus in the Sermon on the Mount. It was part of a trilogy of service. On one side was almsgiving; the center was prayer; on the other side fasting. I further noticed that each of these services was to be done before God in secret.

That thine alms may be in secret. . . .

Matthew 6:4

. . . when thou prayest, enter into thy closet, and when thou hast shut the door, pray to thy Father which is in secret. . . .

Matthew 6:6

. . . when thou fastest . . . appear not unto men to fast, but unto thy Father which is in secret: and thy Father, which seeth in secret, shall reward thee openly.

Matthew 6:17, 18

One truth stood out. God blesses the man who has entered into a personal relationship with Him and preserves this intimacy with care. In giving alms, he dispenses with fanfare, knowing his Father is aware of all his actions. In prayer, he exposes himself to God in a way that would be impossible publicly. In fasting, he realizes that no one but God is to know what he is doing and why. Evidently, a person is to focus his attention on the Lord while performing these services and upon no one else.

## Jesus Fasted

I further was made aware of the fact that Jesus expected us to fast. There is no debating this. Jesus simply said:

Moreover when ye fast. . . .

Matthew 6:16

Jesus lived by His own rules; He fasted.

At first this seemed strange to me. Why would Jesus fast? I also had problems sorting out the reason He would fast at the time He did.

Jesus began His ministry following His water baptism by John the Baptist and the infilling of the Holy Spirit as the dove came out of the heavens and lighted upon Him. But ministry did not begin until He was led into the wilderness by the Holy Spirit to be tempted by Satan. During the forty days of temptation, He fasted.

And Jesus being full of the Holy Ghost returned from Jordan, and was led by the Spirit into the wilderness, being forty days tempted of the devil. And in those days he did eat nothing: and when they were ended, he afterward hungered.

Luke 4:1,2

Why fast immediately following your baptism in water and Spirit? This should have been one of the spiritual pinnacles of Jesus' life! God the Father was with Him and in Him; why fast?

Jesus was fasting secretly before the Father because He needed the Father's strength and determination. He knew the purpose He was to fulfill on the earth. He was born to die as a ransom for sin. He was focusing His attention on the Father. He must not allow His eyes to stray and become captivated by the offers of Satan. He could not afford even to consider shortcut alternatives to the setting up of His Kingdom. He had come to do the Father's will.

Fasting and prayer seemed to strengthen Jesus, for when His time of temptation and fasting was ended, He manifested a new adequacy and poise.

> And Jesus returned in the power of the Spirit into Galilee. . . .
>
> Luke 4:14

The ministry of Jesus among the people then began in earnest. Fasting had accomplished something. I felt I must know more about this.

# 2

# Fasting Is a Focus of Heart

The focus away from food to God which we accomplish in fasting is deliberate. It is our choice not to eat in order to put our attention upon something more important to us. This simple meaning of fasting is expressed by the Greek word *nesteia* which is made up of two parts: the negative prefix *ne* and the verb *esthio*, to eat. In most instances it is translated as voluntary abstinence from food.

Two Hebrew words refer to the practice of fasting. The first simply means "to withhold all natural food from the body." The other describes the effects of fasting as "affliction of soul." Together they convey the thought of voluntary deprivation of the body, subordinating the soul for spiritual purposes.

Fasting has long been known as a means for intensifying prayer. Examples of those who have found spiritual value during times set apart for prayer and fasting are numerous both in Scripture and throughout church history. Those who knew the secrets of fasting as a vital dimension in God included: Jesus Himself, the Apostle Paul, the early church leaders, Isaiah, Daniel, Esther, David, Hannah, Elijah, Ezra, Nehemiah, Zechariah and others. Prominent fasters in the annals of church history include Martin Luther, John Calvin, John Knox, John Wesley, David Brainard, George Müller, Rees

Howells, and many more.

These men and women discovered that abstaining from natural food not only freed them to focus upon God with fresh intensity, but opened avenues of spiritual perception and understanding that were not available during the rush of routine living. They found as they focused upon God by deliberate discipline, God focused upon them in clarity of direction and quickening of spirit. They could partake of God more easily with all else set aside.

> Thy words were found, and I did eat them; and thy
> word was unto me the joy and rejoicing of mine heart:
> for I am called by thy name, O Lord God of hosts.
>
> Jeremiah 15:16

During times alone with God we are able to position our hearts before Him at the exact focal length which will cause spiritual reality to converge upon us. God is always calling us to deeper fellowship and closer communion with Himself, but for the most part our daily routine of activity and social interaction keeps His call from attention. During times of fasting, however, other calls are temporarily suspended and we allow ourselves to be drawn into His presence.

God's call is His initiative. Our response is to deliberately determine to disrupt our busy schedule to make more time for Him. Disruption of the meal schedule usually means that we are willing to set aside all else which would interfere with seeking God wholeheartedly. Eating symbolizes that which is most essential to us. By setting this aside to seek God, we are declaring that He is more important and essential than anything else. Job expressed this determination to seek God with these words:

> . . . I have esteemed the words of his mouth more than
> my necessary food.

Job 23:12

The phrase *necessary food* is better translated "prescribed portion." Job was substituting God for his daily allotment of food. Such a choice is a declaration to let nothing matter more to us than the presence and Word of God.

Physical fasting often introduces further changes into our routine, as they are needed for a particular time of waiting upon God in private with our hearts and souls laid bare before Him. In addition to abstaining from food, we often must refrain from our usual distractions of thought and emotion. We must set aside our habitual ways of doing things in order to gain the most benefit from our time before the Lord.

## God Sees in Secret

Jesus taught that if we fast in secret, God will do a work in our hearts; He will reward us openly. If our focus upon God in fasting is to result in a corresponding focusing of God upon us, He must see our fasting in secret. He is looking upon our heart and examining our inner attitudes and motivation.

The Father is looking at what we do in secret in order to determine how to reward us. We must come apart and do our fasting alone and in private where we will not be tempted to influence the opinions of others. We must shut the door and be direct with God. Here we can afford to be ourselves with

God. Here we must open the secret place of the heart to God. The only place which is truly secret is the inner citadel of our heart and spirit. The secret place is the spiritual realm described by the psalmist:

> He that dwelleth in the secret place of the most High shall abide under the shadow of the Almighty.
>
> Psalms 91:1

God is Spirit and He responds to what we do "in spirit and in truth." He sees what we do in the secret response of our spirit and then rewards us accordingly.

As we focus upon God through prayer and fasting, He looks upon our hearts with increased attention. He examines our motivation. He wants to know whether we are fasting "unto Him." He does not look at the outward aspects of the fasting or even count the meals we have missed. These are merely aids to our personal discipline and focus of heart. He looks at intention.

> . . . for the Lord seeth not as man seeth; for man looketh on the outward appearance, but the Lord looketh on the heart.
>
> 1 Samuel 16:7

But many of the religious people of Jesus' day had forgotten how to be real with God. Their religion consisted of public show. Their acts of devotion were intended to impress others and to build their own image of themselves as pious people. They dressed and acted in ways which would project themselves as deeply religious and to be admired. But in it all they failed to relate to God at all and became dishonest with themselves. Jesus' rebuke was emphatic:

> Moreover when ye fast, be not, as the hypocrites, of a sad countenance: for they disfigure their faces, that they may appear unto men to fast. Verily I say unto you, They have their reward. But thou, when thou fastest, anoint thine head, and wash thy face; That thou appear not unto men to fast, but unto thy Father which is in secret: and thy Father, which seeth in secret, shall reward thee openly.

> Matthew 6:16-18

After awhile, these people were so impressed with themselves and their religious actions that they even sought to impress God. They exaggerated the supposed effects of fasting by refusing to groom themselves. Their religious substitutes for reality with God were making them more self-centered. Everything they did shouted, "Look at me!"

Anything which distracts our focus while we are fasting distorts its purpose. Indeed anything in religion which falls short of heart-to-heart relationship with God has missed its intended goal. The essence of Christianity is oneness of heart with the Lord God. Anything less not only misses the mark, but is in the way and hinders our fellowship.

It is the easiest thing in the world for us to reduce everything we do to its outward or social meanings. We mistake the externals for the realities behind what is visible. If we are not careful, we lose track of our own hearts in the maze of outward activities which appear to serve God but which in fact do not relate to Him.

As soon as our religion ceases to relate directly to God, it becomes sad and wearisome. Our hearts were made to enjoy God. They flourish in His presence. Nothing else can satisfy them. When the heart is not being saturated with His presence, it begins to show signs of homesickness. This sadness shows in the countenance, attitudes, and even the conditions of our bodies.

When our focus of heart is right, all is well with us. When it is not, this too shows all over. David knew this principle well. He said:

> I have set the Lord always before me: because he is at my right hand, I shall not be moved. Therefore my heart is glad, and my glory rejoiceth: my flesh also shall rest in hope. Thou wilt shew me the path of life: in thy presence is fulness of joy; at thy right hand there are pleasures for evermore.
>
> Psalms 16:8, 9, 11

David's focus was right: the Lord was always set before him. His whole being responded with delight. Not only did his heart relax in the glad knowledge of God's loving presence; his tongue rejoiced and his physical body felt the release of hope. It is meant to be this way. God is our well-being. When we are rightly focused on Him, all else falls into right perspective. The balanced life which flows from this right focus is rightly called the *path of life*. It is a path full of joy because He is right there with us.

Since fasting is to be a focus upon God, it is to result in joy.
So the prophet declared:

> Thus saith the Lord of hosts; The fast of the fourth
> month, and the fast of the fifth, and the fast of the
> seventh, and the fast of the tenth, shall be to the house
> of Judah joy and gladness, cheerful feasts; therefore love
> the truth and peace.

Zechariah 8:19

## The Sermon on the Mount

That fasting is a normal part of our walk with God is taken
for granted by the Lord Jesus. Immediately following the
Lord's Prayer, He said:

> Moreover when ye fast. . . .

Matthew 6:16

The context of this discussion is important. In the Sermon
on the Mount Jesus outlined in detail the balanced life. God
is central, and all we do springs from our heart-relationship
with Him. Jesus summed up the life of godly maturity as one
where all issues of life were decided in the heart and performed
with a view to pleasing God rather than ourselves or others.

> Be ye therefore perfect, even as your Father which is
> in heaven is perfect.

Matthew 5:48

Having established by several specific examples that all life must be decided according to spiritual realities, Jesus proceeded to divide all actions into three major categories. These were: doing good to others (almsgiving), intimate relationship to God (prayer), and personal discipline (fasting is used as illustrative of the larger area of self-control). Jesus taught that life in His Kingdom required the right balance among these areas of involvement.

Through the history of the church, however, we see one or another of these areas overemphasized at the expense of the others. The modernistic or social-action churches have enlarged almsgiving in its various forms until it appears to be their whole gospel. For them, the purpose of religion is to rightly relate to our fellow men. The fundamental or Bible churches major on the theme of individual response to God. For them, believing the Word and praying are all important. The Catholic, Episcopal and Lutheran emphasis has been traditionally upon self-discipline and mortification of desires which war against the soul. Fasting has held a prominent role.

Jesus taught the interrelatedness of these three expressions of Christian life. Each is an aid to the others, and together they rightly relate us to God, to others, and to ourselves. But it is characteristic of fallen man to be unable to walk a balanced life in harmony with God. We needed complete salvation, a new birth. Having become the children of God, we must learn how to walk. This can only be achieved by obedience.

The Lord Jesus gave us clear directions to obey concerning almsgiving, prayer, and fasting. Our obedience will bring us into a walk of balance. The directions may be summarized as follows:

1. All you do unto God must be done in secret. Avoid exhibitionism. This applies equally to almsgiving, to prayer, and to fasting.

If we aim our actions at pleasing people, this is all the benefit we can expect. A prayer prayed for men's ears never reaches God. The only answer we have to that prayer is the applause or criticism of men. But prayers from the heart which are addressed only to God have results beyond what we can ask or even imagine. Alms given to be seen of men similarly lose their effectiveness. Fasting done to impress others is likewise vain.

2. Do not copy those who emphasize outward means. Avoid externalism. We must remember that the real work of almsgiving, prayer, and fasting is inward.

It is not the actions others can observe that produce power, but the unseen contact of Spirit with spirit. Publicity detracts from almsgiving. Repetition dilutes petition. Neglect of appearance and bodily care destroys the purpose of fasting.

3. Expect results from God because He rewards the obedient. Obey in faith. God never asks us to do anything just to be doing it. He has a definite purpose in mind and work to accomplish in us through almsgiving, through prayer, and through fasting. If we do these things according to His directions, we will experience His intended results.

Our walk should advertise the truth about God and the joy of serving Him. Consequently, we should let life on the outside seem to be as normal as possible while our fasting is inward unto God. He sees; He will respond.

## Fast Unto the Lord

Zechariah captured the essence of fasting as unto the Lord.

> Then came the word of the Lord of hosts unto me,
> saying, Speak unto all the people of the land, and to the
> priests, saying, When ye fasted and mourned in the
> fifth and seventh month . . . did ye at all fast unto me,
> even to me? And when ye did eat, and when ye did
> drink, did not ye eat for yourselves, and drink for your-
> selves? Should ye not hear the words which the Lord
> hath cried by the former prophets, when Jerusalem was
> inhabited and in prosperity, and the cities thereof
> round about her . . . ?
>
> Zechariah 7:4-7

Focus was the issue, whether they were fasting or eating.
The one question God asked about their fasting was this: Did
you fast unto Me? Did the fast spring from obedience or was
it self-imposed for your own ends?

What focuses our hearts upon God but the Word sent in the
power of His Spirit? God speaks. We hear and our attention
is arrested. We stop and let Him work that Word into our
inner life and write it in the fleshy tables of our hearts.

Unless we are responding from the heart to a word from
God, our fasting will be motivated by self-interest. It may look
like dedicated religion, but the motive of our hearts will be to
please ourselves. This is one of the distinctions between religion and genuine response to God. Religion is doing things to
enhance ourselves; response to God is spontaneous giving of
ourselves in loving obedience. But we cannot respond to God

unless He takes the initiative toward us. The mistake of religion is in trying to duplicate actions we do when responding to God at times when God is not initiating. Fasting is not excepted from this error.

Let me give you two examples.

Repentance is a gift of response to the conviction of the Holy Spirit. But much religion seeks to whip us into a state of sorrow and regret over what we are and what we have been. When we try to make ourselves repent at times that the Holy Spirit is not moving upon our hearts, we end up with all sorts of religious ordeals and practices of penance. But when the Holy Spirit sends a pointed word to our hearts and we know exactly what God expects of us, then we can respond by turning to Him. And in turning to God, we turn away from sin and from our own ways.

Faith too is a gift of response. It is the capacity to hear with the heart what God is saying and to lay hold of it with obedience. By faith we call back to God that which He has first placed in our hearts. Our confession is born of the inworked persuasion of faith. Our heart has heard.

In other words, we can only respond when God takes the initiative. This is the key to any obedience, to any attempt to please God. Fasting is no exception. For a fast to have spiritual value to God or to us, it must be the expressed response of our hearts focused on Him.

## True Fasting Works Change

Fasting which is a response to God's initiative will result in practical outreach. It will make us sensitive on the inside to the needs of others because the shift of focus will free us from self-preoccupation. We will respond to the need we see not only to God in prayer but in caring for others. Zechariah continues:

> And the word of the Lord came unto Zechariah, saying, Thus speaketh the Lord of hosts, saying, Execute true judgment, and shew mercy and compassions every man to his brother: And oppress not the widow, nor the fatherless, the stranger, nor the poor; and let none of you imagine evil against his brother in your heart.
>
> Zechariah 7:8-10

Prayer, alms, fasting—if done with the heart focused on God —will change our hearts. We will not only be moved toward God, but toward our brother. Likewise, if we shut our hearts to God, we will become calloused toward the concerns of others—and vice versa. Eventually we will become unable to respond to God or others. Our religion then is nothing but going through motions and mouthing empty words. God will not give us His attention unless our hearts are right.

> But they refused to hearken, and pulled away the shoulder, and stopped their ears, that they should not hear. Yea, they made their hearts as an adamant stone, lest they should hear the law, and the words which the Lord of hosts hath sent in his spirit by the former prophets: therefore came a great wrath from the Lord of hosts. Therefore it is come to pass, that as he cried, and they would not hear; so they cried, and I would not hear, saith the Lord of hosts.
>
> Zechariah 7:11-13

Because they would not allow their hearts to be focused on God, God allowed them to be scattered by the whirlwind of His wrath. Their religion—even their fasting—did not save them because it was not with an open and responsive heart. Their fasting was not unto God but for selfish ends. Their dead forms failed them and they were left desolate.

Should we not heed this warning of Zechariah and learn to fast unto God?

# 3

# Fasting Is Rest

One great hindrance to focus on God is restlessness caused by anxiety and occupation with the many cares of ordinary life. We are bound by our routine of living. To maintain our focus of heart we must discover fasting as a part of the rhythm of life. It is a rest.

In the case of Martha, eating and entertaining demonstrated her anxiety and restless labor. Mary chose the better part by making her priority fellowship with the Lord (*see* Luke 10:38-42). There are times to eat, and times to share our joys with others; there are also times to rest—physically, emotionally, and socially.

Jesus recognized our need for rest, but He also knew that discipline was required if we were to experience rest. Hear His call:

> Come unto me, all ye that labour and are heavy laden, and I will give you rest. Take my yoke upon you, and learn of me; for I am meek and lowly in heart: and ye shall find rest unto your souls. For my yoke is easy, and my burden is light.

> Matthew 11:28-30

Notice especially what part of us needs the rest. It is in our souls that we are promised rest—rest from our emotions, attitudes and habits. Such rest usually requires freedom to vary our routines so that our emotions are not tied up with our circumstances. One of the most fixed boundaries in the daily schedule concerns eating. Family life is often built around mealtimes.

It is also in connection with meals that we often are engaged in emotional strain and social interaction. God meant it to be, so that mealtimes would be times of fellowship. But unless all those involved are happy and walking in the Spirit, fellowship is not always free from trouble. It can be the time when mother tells dad why Johnny needs to be spanked. It may be the time that Sue clobbers her younger sister for listening on the other extension to that hour-long call from Harold. It may also be the time that mother picks to insist on a new vacuum cleaner. But dad is waiting his turn to announce the raising of union dues, the beginning of a three-week business trip, and the worst score at the golf course since last year.

Agitation during mealtime has long been cited as a major source of indigestion. Yet today if the family is together at all, it is usually around the table. All too frequently, families do not even have time to eat together every day. Tensions mount until the next time they are all together at the table. Angry words have to be digested along with the macaroni.

There are times to come away from it all and be quiet. Here we can find ourselves and God. Then we can go back to each other with a refreshed attitude and perspective.

Spiritual rest very often accompanies physical rest, if we have learned to quiet our thoughts and emotions as well. If we use the physical discipline of abstaining from food and other stimulation, our spirits may be assisted in relaxing before God.

We can then receive refreshing and strength from this time of waiting upon God, as Isaiah promised:

> But they that wait upon the Lord shall renew their strength; they shall mount up with wings as eagles; they shall run, and not be weary; and they shall walk, and not faint.
>
> Isaiah 40:31

When the body is absorbed in digesting food, it is not at its peak. Our systems were designed to have periodic rest and for moderation as a regular rule. But today's pace is such that we often are forced to eat too fast and to overeat some kinds of things while neglecting others. Our diets are rarely disciplined and complete rest from food, even for short periods, is rare indeed. Nevertheless, the benefits of periodic rest are well known both to the medical profession and to spiritual leaders. We need changes in the routine of life; we need the rhythm of rest and activity.

Seasoned prayer warriors have long asserted that rest from food is mandatory if we are to fully concentrate upon God. Andrew Murray so writes in *With Christ in the School of Prayer.*

And *prayer needs fasting* for its full growth. . . . Prayer is the one hand with which we grasp the invisible; fasting, the other, with which we let loose and cast away the visible. In nothing is man more closely connected with the world of sense than in his need of food, and his enjoyment of it.

Focus upon God, who is Spirit, often requires rest from the natural demands upon our bodies, energies and time.

## The Day of Atonement

The Mosaic law took account of our need for variety in routine. A special day was set aside to do no work and to fast. The reason for this was to free people from daily cares and family responsibilities so that they could deal with the inner life of the soul.

> And this shall be a statute for ever unto you: that in the seventh month, on the tenth day of the month, ye shall afflict your souls, and do no work at all, whether it be one of your own country, or a stranger that sojourneth among you: For on that day shall the priest make an atonement for you, to cleanse you, that ye may be clean from all your sins before the Lord. It shall be a sabbath of rest unto you, and ye shall afflict your souls, by a statute for ever.
>
> Leviticus 16:29-31

*Afflicting the soul* was another term for fasting. This was a time to deprive the natural appetites and turn attention inward to more pressing needs. In order to rest from daily chores and change the routine, eating had to be set aside for that day. So long as meals have to be served, some people cannot rest from their daily activities. If all were to rest, the meal schedule needed to be suspended.

But the meaning of the fasting went deeper than this. They were to afflict their souls by denying themselves the usual

comforts and distractions of eating. They were to face themselves before God without the natural escape routes such as
eating. Furthermore, they were to allow themselves to feel
sorrow for their sin and to express it. Fasting and weeping were
to express that sorrow. It was a time for honest emotion.

> When I wept, and chastened my soul with fasting,
> that was to my reproach. I made sackcloth also my gar-
> ment. . . .
>
> Psalms 69:10, 11

We often have to set aside all usual activities before we can
face ourselves. Our busy schedules which clamor that they are
necessary are also escapes from inner honesty. When we do not
want to know what is in our hearts, we get too busy. We crowd
out self-awareness with the feeling that we are busy about
important business. But when we are too busy to be real with
ourselves, we cannot be personal in our relationships to others.
Even our religious work degenerates into impersonal function-
ing. We must allow time to keep in touch with ourselves and
to pour out our hearts to God. Rest is essential. Fasting secures
it.

The Hebrew word for sabbath means rest. The Day of
Atonement was a "sabbath of rest." It was a rest from even the
most basic routines. It was a call to full halt in order that God
might have complete attention.

Why was such a demand made upon God's people? God
needed their attention in order to make them fully aware of
their inner need and of His provision. God was revealing His
hatred for sin and the cost of cleansing. He needed their entire

focus as He demonstrated redemption. No wonder it was a serious offense to be found involved in any other activity at this time.

> And ye shall do no work in that same day: for it is a day of atonement, to make an atonement for you before the Lord your God. For whatsoever soul it be that shall not be afflicted in that same day, he shall be cut off from among his people. And whatsoever soul it be that doeth any work in that same day, the same soul will I destroy from among his people. Ye shall do no manner of work: it shall be a statute for ever throughout your generations in all your dwellings. It shall be unto you a sabbath of rest, and ye shall afflict your souls: in the ninth day of the month at even, from even unto even, shall ye celebrate your sabbath.
>
> Leviticus 23:28-32

This was the only one of Israel's holidays that was celebrated with a fast. But the affliction of soul was essential to mark the importance of sin and its covering. They had to stop and take notice of what God was doing. The high priest was not just making atonement for his own sin; he was representing the whole nation. The people had to be involved. Their continued welfare depended upon God's acceptance of the annual offering for sin. This day of fasting was intended to call attention to the solemnity and significance of the sprinkling of blood upon the mercy seat.

Arnold D. Peisker in *Wesleyan Bible Commentary* describes the importance of this day.

It was to be the climactic event in Jewish expiatory ceremonials. In the events of this day all the lesser acts of atonement culminated. While the holiness of God and the sinfulness of sin are set forth, special stress is laid here upon the completeness of the pardon offered to the sinner and his restoration to divine favor. This was to be a day in which Israel was to give its most solemn expression of repentance, faith and worship. . . . This was a day in which Israelites, characteristically arrogant and self-willed . . . were to humble themselves before the Lord. As an outward indication of their inward sorrow and penitence, the people were to spend the day in fasting. It came, in fact, to be referred to as "the fast" (cf. Acts 27:9).

Some have called the Day of Atonement the "Good Friday of the Old Testament." This is quite appropriate, for on Good Friday sin was dealt with by one offering—an offering which would never have to be repeated. Jesus Christ was both our High Priest and the perfect Lamb of God to take away all sin forever, and to mediate a New Covenant between God and man.

But the lesson of fasting in order to rest and to give God our attention continues to be valid. While we no longer celebrate a Day of Atonement, we do periodically stop to remember His sacrifice for our sins and to reapply His benefits to ourselves by faith and partaking of the Lord's Supper.

Here at the Lord's Supper we find a similar admonition to stop and look at ourselves. We must call a halt to our frantic activity and examine ourselves in the light of His Word and with the help of the Spirit. Is there unconfessed sin? Are amends needed? Does communication with our brother need improvement? Are we in the faith?

Self-examination is an important aspect of afflicting our

souls. Indeed, this is probably the main reason for such a practice. Fasting often is a real help in quieting us from the usual bustle and in setting aside time for self-examination. Fasting therefore became associated with the Lord's Supper during the early history of the church and is still practiced in some churches as a means of preparation for receiving the communion.

## Labor to Enter Into Rest

The Old Covenant sabbath is carried over into the New Covenant in the rest we find in Christ. It is no longer a special day or an outward observance; it is a condition of heart. Indeed it is a rest still promised to us.

> There remaineth therefore a rest [keeping of sabbath] to the people of God. For he that is entered into his rest, he also hath ceased from his own works, as God did from his. Let us labour therefore to enter into that rest, lest any man fall after the same example of unbelief.
>
> Hebrews 4:9-11

The key to rest is faith. Only when we are given the ability to believe can we rest from our many attempts to do something to influence God. Fasting, like other prayer practices, can be another form of our own works. It can hinder our rest because it expresses our unbelief.

It is not what we do or not do which keeps us from rest. It is our attitude of heart. Unbelief provokes God to wrath and to a determination to prevent our entering into rest. Indeed, unbelief is called *an evil heart* because it makes us depart from God. Faith, on the other hand, is itself the entrance to rest.

> So I sware in my wrath, They shall not enter into my rest. Take heed, brethren, lest there be in any of you an evil heart of unbelief, in departing from the living God.
>
> Hebrews 3:11, 12

> For we which have believed do enter into rest, as he said, As I have sworn in my wrath, if they shall enter into my rest: although the works were finished from the foundation of the world.
>
> Hebrews 4:3

The main symptom of unbelief is restlessness. The unbelieving heart drives us to take on a million projects and to make them the means of getting somewhere with God. But the characteristic of faith is contentment in the knowledge that God takes the initiative toward us. We need only be open and available to Him.

## Fasting Is a Work of Faith

When we pray and fast unto God, we are acting upon a basic trust that God will honor us. We are motivated by an expectancy that we will meet Him. If we seek Him, we will find Him.

Fasting in particular expresses confidence in nothing else but the Lord. It is a shift of focus from the temporal, seen securities to the spiritual as truly lasting. We are not clinging in dependence to the earthly, but we are putting our full weight down

upon the God of our salvation. This dependency upon God is
a response of faith created in our hearts by God.

David understood the necessity of renouncing all reliance
upon other sources and expecting all from God.

> Truly my soul waiteth upon God: from him cometh my
> salvation. He only is my rock and my salvation; he is my
> defence; I shall not be greatly moved. My soul, wait
> thou only upon God; for my expectation is from him.
> He only is my rock and my salvation: he is my defence;
> I shall not be moved. In God is my salvation and my
> glory: the rock of my strength, and my refuge, is in
> God.
>
> Psalms 62:1, 2, 5-7

Fasting from our regular food expresses our refusal to depend
upon our familiar routines, schedules, and natural nourishment. We tell our hearts by these deliberate actions that we
have determined to rely only upon God. By periodically refusing to continue in our rut of routine eating, we communicate
deeply to ourselves that we do not live by bread alone. Instead
we abstain from food to remind ourselves that we live by that
manna which comes down from above.

It is faith that makes the difference between fasting as a
form, or even as self-punishment, and fasting as a vehicle of
prayer. In a true fast our expectation is upon God rather than
upon the fast itself.

I have read a great deal of literature which promises all sorts
of benefits to those who will fast. The longer the fast, the more
severe the deprivation, the greater the results, they say. But

they do not focus upon God or set their expectation upon Him. Instead their reliance is on the act of fasting. The fast itself is to produce all the benefits. The means has become the end and God has been lost in the mechanics of abstaining from food. This is not faith; it is idolatry, for it puts confidence in the relative instead of in God, the absolute.

Fasting itself will rest the physical body. Fasting in faith unto God will also rest the soul and unclutter the spirit. Should we not labor to enter into all the rest God has provided by faith?

# 4

# How Should We Fast?

"A fast is of little value unless you drink only water."

"This is not true. I know a person who fasted for ten days and drank soup most of the time. Fasting made a difference in his life."

"The only thing I know about fasting is that during Lent we abstained from things, not so much food. Oh, yes, we did stop eating meat."

"You are all wrong. When we fasted, we left off eating one meal a day. This is the right way to fast."

The above remarks were part of a discussion during a recent religious convention. Somehow fasting entered the conversation and each person was off and running. I listened intently. When the conversation ended, nothing had been clarified to anyone.

What about it? What does the Bible say about the ways of fasting? Does it speak clearly on this point?

Yes, the Bible speaks with some clarity, but more by inference and example than by actual command. Some persons observed a total fast, others a normal fast, and yet others fasts of varying degrees. Each was honored by the Lord when his motive was to seek God.

Since the word *fast* means not eating, its basic application is simple abstinence from food. We cannot spiritualize this any more than we can spiritualize the water in water baptism or the elements of the Lord's Supper. It is sometimes necessary to abstain from entertainment and from things in addition to food in order to achieve focus on God. To understand Scripture correctly, we must use words the way they were intended. Nevertheless, even within the area of abstinence from food there is considerable controversy. We must clarify the kinds of fasting illustrated in Scripture.

## The Total Fast

The total fast is one of complete abstinence from food and water. There are a few examples in the Bible, but the total fast must be approached with caution. A person can live for many days without food, depending on his weight, size, and general health. But he can only live a few days without water.

The examples we have in Scripture seem to indicate that the total fast should not exceed three days. Saul of Tarsus fasted totally for three days and three nights following his confrontation with the Lord Jesus on the Damascus road.

> And Saul arose from the earth; and when his eyes were opened, he saw no man: but they led him by the hand, and brought him into Damascus. And he was three days without sight, and neither did eat nor drink.
>
> Acts 9:8, 9

Please bear in mind that Saul did not plan ahead to fast for this three-day and three-night period; the fast grew out of crisis. The desire for food and drink seems to diminish when we are in deep distress. Saul was waiting in total blindness for further instructions from the Lord. It was a time of complete upheaval and reversal of life purposes. His anxiety must have been extreme during this time of reorientation.

Another clear account of people fasting totally for three days and nights is found in the Book of Esther. Queen Esther faced the most difficult moment of her life. She had determined to initiate an audience with the king to intercede for her people, the Jews. This unsolicited intrusion into the king's presence could cost her life. Consequently, she spoke with Mordecai:

> . . . hold a fast on my behalf, and neither eat nor drink
> for three days, night or day. I and my maids will also
> fast as you do. . . .
>
> Esther 4:16 RSV

One more example of the total fast in Scripture was also occasioned by overwhelming emotion. This is found when Ezra was so disturbed by the sin of his countrymen, that he found no better way to express the intensity of his grief and sorrow.

> Then Ezra . . . did eat no bread, nor drink water: for
> he mourned because of the transgression of them that
> had been carried away.
>
> Ezra 10:6

These total fasts have one element in common: they were intense, but they were brief. They resulted from immediate shock to the whole system; everything was temporarily suspended.

Paul and Ezra fasted on other occasions when such intensity was not present. At those times, they abstained only from food.

## Supernatural Fasts

Three forty-day total fasts are mentioned in Scripture, but each was supernatural. God initiated them and enabled the men to be sustained. These fasts were so beyond the ordinary that we would do well to dismiss any thoughts of duplicating them.

Moses not only fasted from food and water for forty days in order to receive the Commandments in stone, but immediately returned to the mountain for a second forty-day fast when it was necessary to obtain them again. No mention is made of his eating or drinking between these two periods, which were not far apart. He was so deeply distressed over the idolatry of Israel that it is unlikely that the thought of breaking fast even occurred to him during his brief intermission from the mountaintop. His own account reads:

> When I was gone up into the mount to receive the tables of stone, even the tables of the covenant which the Lord made with you, then I abode in the mount forty days and forty nights, I neither did eat bread nor drink water. So I turned and came down from the mount, and the mount burned with fire: and the two tables of the covenant were in my two hands. And I looked, and, behold, ye had sinned against the Lord your God, and had made you a molten calf: ye had turned aside quickly out of the way which the Lord had commanded you. And I took the two tables, and cast

them out of my two hands, and brake them before your
eyes. And I fell down before the Lord, as at the first,
forty days and forty nights: I did neither eat bread, nor
drink water, because of all your sins which ye sinned,
in doing wickedly in the sight of the Lord, to provoke
him to anger.

Deuteronomy 9:9, 15-18

Taking the whole context of this story, we must consider
that these two fasts were part of the phenomena of this special
event in history. We do not expect a repetition of the mount
burning with fire or of God writing in stone; we need not
expect a duplication of these forty-day total fasts.

The third forty-day fast from food and water mentioned in
Scripture is that of Elijah after his confrontation with the
prophets of Baal when he journeyed to Mount Horeb. (This,
by the way, is the same mountain Moses climbed; they are two
names for the same place.) The whole context of Elijah's fast
is also supernatural.

Before undertaking the journey and the fast, Elijah was
awakened by the touch of an angel. Twice at the insistent
bidding of the angel, he ate a cake and drank water. This food
was to strengthen him for the coming journey of forty days and
nights. Obviously only divine intervention made such suste-
nance possible.

And he arose, and did eat and drink, and went in the
strength of that meat forty days and forty nights unto
Horeb the mount of God.

1 Kings 19:8

Elijah's confrontation with the Lord in the mount was out of the ordinary. Again we must consider the total fast of such a length as phenomenal.

Arthur Wallis interprets these fasts as supernatural in *God's Chosen Fast.*

A journey of such duration through the burning desert, if it was completed, as Scripture implies, without further nourishment, constitutes an absolute fast quite as supernatural as those of Moses. If that be so, it is another striking parallel between these two leading representatives of the old covenant, Moses the giver of the law, and Elijah its restorer . . . for both had a supernatural ending to their earthly course, as well as a supernatural re-appearance with Christ on the holy mount.

Leaving aside such fasts as these which were epoch-making and supernatural, we conclude that the absolute fast is an exceptional measure for an exceptional situation.

## The Normal Fast

The normal fast is simply a complete abstinence from food. Water is taken. Jesus fasted for forty days, but He did not abstain from water. His fast was unusually long, but it was not a total fast.

Being forty days tempted of the devil. And in those days he did eat nothing: and when they were ended, he afterward hungered.

Luke 4:2

There is no indication that He did not drink anything. The Scriptures tell us that after His fast He was hungry, but no mention is made of thirst. His temptation was to make bread from the stones, not to cause water to gush out of them.

Water is essential to maintain normal body functions; it is vital to life. God does not expect us to endanger our health by unwisely abstaining from water. Most of the Bible fasts were simply abstinence from food for shorter or longer periods, depending on the purpose of the fast.

## Fasts of Varying Degrees

The persons already mentioned who engaged in fasting were most certainly focusing their attention on the Lord God. This is quite evident. But apparently focus can be achieved by varying degrees of fasting.

Probably the clearest account of a limited or partial fast is recorded in the Book of Daniel and concerns Daniel himself. He fasted in order to maintain his integrity before God by separation.

> But Daniel purposed in his heart that he would not defile himself with the portion of the king's meat, nor with the wine which he drank: therefore he requested of the prince of the eunuchs that he might not defile himself.
>
> Daniel 1:8

In the place of his assigned food and wine, Daniel requested pulse (a vegetable resembling peas and beans). On this limited diet, he gained strength and fitness.

Later on in Daniel's life, he engaged in a three-week fast from pastries, meat, and from wine. God had given him a vision and a burden to pray until it was accomplished, but the opposition was fierce. For twenty-one days Daniel sought God with mourning and fasting, but with still no apparent results. Was his fast too limited? Had he diluted its effectiveness by not refusing all food? No!

An angel personally informed him that from the beginning of his fast, his prayer was effective. He had been heard. Things were set in motion in the heavenlies.

> In those days I Daniel was mourning three full weeks.
> I ate no pleasant bread, neither came flesh nor wine
> into my mouth, neither did I anoint myself at all, till
> three whole weeks were fulfilled. Then said he unto me,
> Fear not, Daniel: for from the first day that thou didst
> set thine heart to understand, and to chasten thyself
> before thy God, thy words were heard, and I am come
> for thy words.
>
> Daniel 10:2, 3, 12

What made Daniel's fast effective according to the angelic messenger was his set of heart or focus. What he ate and what he did not eat was not significant in itself. He abstained as much as was necessary to maintain his focus upon God during those difficult weeks of waiting.

Through these past years, it has been my evaluation that the people who practice fasting in varying ways, depending on their present circumstances, are the more spiritually balanced. There is a reason. They are more sensitive to God and seek to please Him rather than to follow some religious ideas. They have learned the value of frequent exposure to God in fastings.

# 5

# Fasting Is an Honest Reaction

Reactions of intense emotion, such as grief, desperate longing, or anger, affect our digestion. At these times fasting is a natural response. We cannot handle too much emotion and food at the same time. We temporarily refrain from eating.

Intense emotion and sickness affect us in much the same way —we lose our desire for food.

> He is chastened also with pain upon his bed, and the multitude of his bones with strong pain: So that his life abhorreth bread, and his soul dainty meat.
>
> Job 33:19, 20

> My heart is smitten, and withered like grass; so that I forget to eat my bread.
>
> Psalms 102:4

Hannah's distress during her barrenness was expressed not only in her emotions and words but in her eating habits. Her desire for a child had so consumed her that nothing else mattered.

> Then said Elkanah, her husband to her, Hannah, why
> weepest thou? and why eatest thou not? and why is thy
> heart grieved? am not I better to thee than ten sons?
>
> 1 Samuel 1:8

In our day, the open expression of emotion is discouraged—
we are too sophisticated to reveal our hearts. Psychologists tell
us that we lose much creativeness and zest for living for just
this reason: we will not accept ourselves and be honest in our
emotional reactions. We try too hard to convince others that
we are someone other than ourselves, and in so doing we lose
the power to be ourselves. But in Bible days this was not the
case. The Orientals—and this included the Hebrews—had
developed a whole language of gesture, apparel, and outward
signs to show people what they felt inside.

Fasting and several related gestures had specific meaning in
the Hebrew culture. They said something as definite and
unambiguous as spoken words. Take the wearing of sackcloth,
for example.

Rough garments shaped like sacks were made from dark-
colored goat's hair. They were unpleasant both to look at and
to feel against one's skin. People in mourning wore sackcloth
to picture their inner sorrow and displeasure. Eventually the
wearing of sackcloth was inseparably associated with deep mental anguish. Sackcloth was often worn in connection with fasting. Together these outward actions communicated, "My soul
is in trouble."

The prophets understood the language of outward behavior
and often employed the external signs to talk about matters of
the heart.

Tremble, ye women that are at ease; be troubled, ye careless ones: strip you, and make you bare, and gird sackcloth upon your loins.

Isaiah 32:11

For this gird you with sackcloth, lament and howl: for the fierce anger of the Lord is not turned back from us.

Jeremiah 4:8

The wearing of ashes and shaving the head communicated sorrow to the point of shame and deep humiliation. Calamity and disappointment were felt as personal dishonor and expressed as baldness and in wearing ashes upon one's face or head.

They shall also gird themselves with sackcloth, and horror shall cover them; and shame shall be upon all faces, and baldness upon all their heads.

Ezekiel 7:18

And Tamar put ashes on her head, and rent her garment of divers colours that was on her, and laid her hand on her head, and went on crying.

2 Samuel 13:19

The fact that behavior is language is well known to linguists and anthropologists. The customs of various cultures communicate as clearly as words and grammar. But language, whether of word or action, can lose its power to communicate honestly—true meaning can be detached from the symbols. What is expressed outwardly can fail to show what is on the inside.

In other words, language can be used either to communicate or to miscommunicate. It can either reveal or hide the true contents of the heart.

For example, Joab skillfully used the outward garb of mourning as well as deceitful words to induce David to return Absalom from exile.

> And Joab sent to Tekoah, and fetched thence a wise woman, and said unto her, I pray thee, feign thyself to be a mourner, and put on now mourning apparel, and anoint not thyself with oil, but be as a woman that had a long time mourned for the dead: And come to the king and speak on this manner unto him. So Joab put the words in her mouth.
>
> 2 Samuel 14:2, 3

Not only did Joab put words in her mouth, he told her how to dress and how to deport herself to pretend a state of emotion. He coached her as an actress portraying the mourning widow. This would not have been possible had the culture not developed common meanings for costume and gestures.

Such deliberate misuse of behavior and language was condemned by Jesus as hypocrisy. In fact, the Greek word *hypokrites* means "play-actor". The Greek and Roman dramatists were noted for their use of large masks and mechanical devices to convey emotion. A hypocrite, in the scriptural sense, is one who uses outward forms of communication to cover up inner reality. He is saying something on the outside which is not true in the heart.

Language in itself, whether verbal or nonverbal, is neither true nor untrue; it depends upon our use of it. Fasting and its related customs could either express the heart or be used hypocritically. Honest fasting was a direct, spontaneous reaction felt in the body as well as the soul. It was a true emotional response which said, "I cannot eat; what I am feeling inside matters too much." The intensity of the emotion determined the extent and duration of the fasting.

Jonathan was angered by his father's rejection of David to the point that hunger left him. Who could eat when his father had thrown a javelin at his best friend! Jonathan's distress consumed him; he fasted.

> So Jonathan arose from the table in fierce anger, and did eat no meat the second day of the month: for he was grieved for David, because his father had done him shame.
>
> 1 Samuel 20:34

In addition to being the natural reaction of distaste for food, Jonathan's fasting was a way of communicating to his father the extent of his displeasure. Mere words and facial expressions were insufficient. Fasting said with power beyond words that Jonathan's heart-response was one of serious concern and deep humiliation. This was an honest fast because it correctly revealed Jonathan's heart, but it was not a spiritual fast because it was not directed toward the Lord.

## David's Honesty

David's occasions for fasting offer much instruction to us, especially when we remember that God considered David a man after His own heart.

David was able to express himself openly and honestly without allowing the culture to stifle him. When returning the ark of God's presence to Jerusalem after many years of neglect, David could translate his joy into dancing in spite of his royal office. He was not ashamed to let his rejoicing be seen, even though his wife was disgusted by his liberty. Likewise, David could weep openly when occasion demanded. He could rend his clothes to represent deep distress, and his mourning on several occasions involved body and soul in fasting. What was in David's heart showed on his face, in his actions, and determined his decisions. Honest reactions were spontaneously expressed without distortion.

David's fasting was part of his honesty. He fasted according to the promptings of his heart and he communicated his true emotions. According to the customs for mourning at the time of death, David fasted.

David's mourning for the death of Saul and of Jonathan included fasting. It is not surprising that the death of one as intimately bound up with him as Jonathan would deeply move David. He could not desire food while the emotions of loss and shock swept over him, so he set aside time for his reactions. He did not try to go on as usual, pretending that he did not care.

Then David took hold on his clothes, and rent them; and likewise all the men that were with him: And they mourned, and wept, and fasted until even, for Saul, and for Jonathan his son, and for the people of the Lord, and for the house of Israel; because they were fallen by the sword.

2 Samuel 1:11, 12

A little later on, David lamented the murder of his friend Abner with fasting.

And when all the people came to cause David to eat meat while it was yet day, David sware, saying, So do God to me, and more also, if I taste bread, or ought else, till the sun be down.

2 Samuel 3:35

Was David honest in mourning the death of Saul when Saul had been seeking his life? Would not Saul's death bring relief to David rather than grief? It is easy to see how fasting and mourning for Jonathan and for Abner were appropriate, but what about his demonstrated grief at the death of Saul? How could he rend his clothes in public and fast for Saul and not be a hypocrite?

The answer to this question is found in Psalms. When David sang songs to the Lord, he sang from the depths of his heart. He put music to words which conveyed the true content of his soul. During one of these times of prayer and singing before the Lord, David recorded words which reveal his capacity to fast for his enemies. These words are found in the context of a complaint because his enemies were not treating David fairly. Nevertheless, David's words clearly show that he was a man of such compassion that he could make his enemies' problems his own and pray accordingly.

> False witnesses did rise up; they laid to my charge things that I knew not. They rewarded me evil for good to the spoiling of my soul. But as for me, when they were sick, my clothing was sackcloth: I humbled my soul with fasting; and my prayer returned into mine own bosom. I behaved myself as though he had been my friend or brother: I bowed down heavily, as one that mourneth for his mother.
>
> Psalms 35:11-14

David loved his enemies, including Saul. He was genuinely sorry to see Saul come to such a pathetic end. His grief was real. His fast was honest.

## Spiritual Honesty

David was so careful to express himself appropriately on all occasions, that his fasting confused his followers on one occasion. The cultural expectation was that fasting should follow the death of a loved one, especially when the person was a member of one's own family. But David fasted first, while there was some faint hope of recovery. When death came, David resumed normal life. What could this mean?

David was expressing something deeper than emotion. He had moved to a spiritual plane. He was talking to God.

The occasion was the most serious crisis David faced during his lifetime. He had committed the serious sins of murder and adultery and now he had been found out. Nathan, the prophet, had exposed him and declared God's judgment against him. The child born of the wife he had stolen from Uriah must die. What a terrible truth this must have been for David to face. God had spoken and the child was dangerously ill. Death was impending.

But David knew God. He knew that above all else, God was merciful. He would forgive sin and restore the sinner. He had learned that God answers prayer and that no honest cry is turned aside. He had further learned that fasting is a language God understands. (It communicates to God that this petition matters so much that one cannot eat until it has been answered. Fasting adds the dimension of focus to prayer; God cannot miss the point.)

David prayed and David fasted for seven days, entreating the Lord to spare the child. This was both an honest fast and a spiritual fast because David was communicating from the heart to the Lord. The depth of his heart-searching before the Lord is preserved for us in Psalms 51 which was written during the time of repentance and humbling himself.

During this time of intense focus upon God, David saw himself as God saw him. God uncovered his heart and David acknowledged his sins. David discovered by experience that God's focus is upon the heart.

> Behold, thou desirest truth in the inward parts: and in the hidden part thou shalt make me to know wisdom. Create in me a clean heart, O God; and renew a right spirit within me.
>
> Psalms 51:6,10

God did not want anything external; He wanted a change in heart.

> For thou desirest not sacrifice; else would I give it: thou delightest not in burnt offering. The sacrifices of God are a broken spirit: a broken and a contrite heart, O God, thou wilt not despise.
>
> Psalms 51:16, 17

These words show us that David did not consider his fasting as a form of sacrifice or as a means of placating God. He knew God too well to think of Him in terms of external religion. David's fasting was simply his honest reaction to the extremity of the situation. Sin was that serious. He had to get alone, set all else aside, and really find God. By fasting, David communicated both to himself and to God, "This is urgent, I am setting my heart to seeking You, Lord."

Nevertheless, the child died. David found repentance and restoration, but God found it necessary to answer David's supplication with a firm *no*. David learned by the hushed demeanor of his servants that the child was dead. He ended his fast and resumed his daily activities, to the puzzlement of all.

> Then said his servants unto him, What thing is this that thou hast done? thou didst fast and weep for the child, while it was alive; but when the child was dead, thou didst rise and eat bread.
>
> 2 Samuel 12:21

The servants were confused by David's seeming impropriety. Here was the occasion for sackcloth, for ashes, for weeping, and for fasting. Here was the time to show others the depth of his grief and disappointment. What would it look like if the king failed to mourn the death of his own son? It was unthinkable! But David had an answer:

> And he said, While the child was yet alive, I fasted and wept: for I said, Who can tell whether God will be gracious to me, that the child may live? But now he is dead, wherefore should I fast? can I bring him back again? I shall go to him, but he shall not return to me.
>
> 2 Samuel 12:22, 23

How much was compacted into the words, *wherefore should I fast?* David had learned something about God and he had learned more about fasting. He had learned to be spiritually honest and direct as well as culturally honest. He had something more important to communicate than sorrow for loss, for God had restored the joy of his salvation. He had been thoroughly cleansed from all his sin and God's presence was again his portion. It was a time for praise.

A few years later, Solomon eloquently described this concept of appropriateness with these poetic words:

> To every thing there is a season, and a time to every purpose under the heaven: A time to be born, and a time to die; a time to plant, and a time to pluck up that which is planted; A time to kill, and a time to heal; a time to break down, and a time to build up; A time to

weep, and a time to laugh; a time to mourn, and a time to dance.

Ecclesiastes 3:1-4

Could we not add: a time to feast, and a time to fast?

# 6

# A Time to Fast?

A time to fast! Is there a right time, or is this a matter for individual decision? Does the church have the right of initiative in calling its people to fast? Should we wait for a directive word from God before we fast? No sooner is the subject of fasting mentioned than questions such as these arise from every side.

This is not a new question. The Pharisees asked it. They observed that in contrast to their own tradition and in contrast to John and his followers, Jesus and His disciples made little room for fasting. The Pharisees wanted to know when Jesus and His disciples would make time for fasting.

> And the disciples of John and of the Pharisees used to fast: and they come and say unto him, Why do the disciples of John and of the Pharisees fast, but thy disciples fast not?
>
> Mark 2:18

> And they said unto him, Why do the disciples of John fast often, and make prayers, and likewise the disciples of the Pharisees; but thine eat and drink?
>
> Luke 5:33

Jesus answered by making timing a question of appropriateness. Fasting was appropriate in times of trouble and loss. He tied fasting to the immediate circumstances, to felt need. It was to be an honest reaction—one growing out of real life. The language of sorrow, trouble, and loss belongs in context. Jesus said:

> . . . Can the children of the bridechamber fast, while the bridegroom is with them? as long as they have the bridegroom with them, they cannot fast. But the days will come when the bridegroom shall be taken away from them, and then shall they fast in those days.
>
> Mark 2:19, 20

Jesus was referring to Himself as the Bridegroom and to His disciples as the children of the bridechamber. He was using the language of appropriateness. Weddings were occasions for festivity and joy. One could not bring the behavior of the funeral procession into such a setting; it was not fitting. Jesus was pointing out that fasting fits certain occasions—the times of calamity, loss, or sorrow. Fasting was to express genuine mourning.

What did Jesus mean when He said, *then shall they fast in those days?* What days was He describing? Many people have interpreted these Scriptures to imply that Christians must fast as a regular practice during this entire period between Jesus' Ascension and His Second Coming. I do not believe He was talking about this time.

The specific period of mourning for His disciples in connection with His departure was the period between His arrest and His Resurrection. The words of John clarify this:

A little while, and ye shall not see me: and again, a little while, and ye shall see me, because I go to the Father. Verily, verily, I say unto you, That ye shall weep and lament, but the world shall rejoice: and ye shall be sorrowful, but your sorrow shall be turned into joy. A woman when she is in travail hath sorrow, because her hour is come: but as soon as she is delivered of the child, she remembereth no more the anguish, for joy that a man is born into the world. And ye now therefore have sorrow: but I will see you again, and your heart shall rejoice, and your joy no man taketh from you.

John 16:16, 20-22

The Bible describes the depression and confusion of the disciples during Jesus' trial, death, and time in the grave. It also describes the joy of His Resurrection.

. . . he shewed unto them his hands and his side. Then were the disciples glad, when they saw the Lord.

John 20:20

He again left them when He ascended into heaven, but this was a different matter. It was an occasion of victory and joy. Luke said:

And it came to pass, while he blessed them, he was parted from them, and carried up into heaven. And they worshipped him, and returned to Jerusalem with

great joy: And were continually in the temple, praising
and blessing God. Amen.

Luke 24:51-53

This does not sound like a time of mourning.

Furthermore, Jesus had promised His disciples that as He
took His place at His Father's right hand, He would send
another Comforter—one just like Him—to take His place.
Their relationship would be even more intimate and complete
than it had become during those three and one-half years of
walking together. Why? The Spirit would come and live on the
inside; He would be closer to them than human limitations had
allowed.

And I will pray the Father, and he shall give you another Comforter, that he may abide with you for ever;
Even the Spirit of truth; whom the world cannot receive, because it seeth him not, neither knoweth him:
but ye know him; for he dwelleth with you, and shall
be in you. I will not leave you comfortless: I will come
to you.

John 14:16-18

In the Book of Acts, Luke described the ministry of the Holy
Spirit as a continuation of the life of Jesus. The Holy Spirit was
a Comforter indeed; God was with them. This age is not a
general period of mourning; it is the age of the Holy Spirit. The
wedding atmosphere ended for the disciples with the death of
Jesus Christ. With the coming of the Holy Spirit they were to
get down to the real business of living. Living includes tribula-
tion and sorrow; they could expect to fast.

## A Time to Mourn?

There are appropriate times for mourning and for fasting. Did not Solomon say, *a time to mourn . . .?*

In the Old Testament, mourning accompanied repentance. Sorrow for sin was to be shown outwardly in apparel, in weeping, in gestures and with fasting. Just as they demonstrated their grief over the death of a loved one, so they were to mourn for their sin.

Mourning was the expected response of all God's creatures whenever He made them aware of His displeasure or wrath. Even the earth languished under the frown of God. Whenever God thundered judgment, the earth trembled in profound lament and deep anguish. The prophetic writings are filled with dramatic scenes of mourning and turning to God in deep sorrow for sin. Even more often, however, God's people were reproved for not mourning at times when judgment was approaching.

Demonstrated repentance often served to avert the judgments of God. When God saw that the people had responded to His warnings by weeping, by fasting, and by determining to change their ways, He would change His mind and either mitigate His punishment or defer it.

God reproves by His Word, but when people will not hear, He sends chastening to make His message clear. When God pleads with people to turn, He may use drastic measures to gain their attention and to create willingness for change. These are times for mourning and for an unreserved seeking of God. When God reproves, it is time to turn to Him with all our heart. If the heart is too cluttered and self-satisfied to turn, it is time to fast.

> Therefore also now, saith the Lord, turn ye even to me
> with all your heart, and with fasting, and with weeping,
> and with mourning.
>
> Joel 2:12

One of the Hebrew words for fasting, you will recall, meant "affliction of soul"—a combination of humbling oneself and mourning. To afflict our soul means to accept responsibility for our own actions instead of putting the blame upon others. We do not bring a situation to God with the complaint, "Look at what they are doing to me. See how unfairly I am being treated. . . ." No! We come with a readiness to be shown where we need change. We ask God, "What am I doing to aggravate this situation? What are You trying to change in me? What am I to learn in this experience?"

Our mourning is both a reaction to God's chastening, and sorrow as God uncovers sin to be confessed and removed. The only way to have debris removed from our inner life is to let God wash it away, and this requires specific acknowledgment on our part.

> If we confess our sins, he is faithful and just to forgive
> us our sins, and to cleanse us from all unrighteousness.
>
> 1 John 1:9

Fasting is not necessary every time we find unconfessed sin. Confession and cleansing should be part of our daily walking in the light.

But there are times that deeper, more thorough self-examination and repentance may be required for us to find

God in the measure we need to find Him. Repeated petition seems unavailing and direction is not forthcoming. We know that we are not penetrating into His presence in our praying. We sense that we are too full of ourselves to really settle down and wait for God. Instead, we are distracted by clutter of every sort. It is time to fast and to let God strip away our hindrances to focus upon Himself.

The link between fasting and affliction of soul or humbling ourselves is clearly stated in the Psalms of David. Compare, for example, these words:

> But as for me, when they were sick, my clothing was sackcloth; I afflicted myself with fasting, and I prayed with head bowed on my breast.
>
> Psalms 35:13 AMPLIFIED

> When I wept *and* humbled myself with fasting, I was jeered at *and* humiliated.
>
> Psalms 69:10 AMPLIFIED

## How Fasting Humbles Us

As we seek to understand the spiritual function of fasting, we must recall that it is affliction of soul, not of the body. Focus upon God is not achieved simply by physical deprivation; it requires the exposure of the heart. Fasting accomplishes this work which we call *humbling ourselves* in several ways.

First of all, fasting is a time for honest self-examination. We set all else aside to free our attention for God. As soon as we discontinue our outward diversions, we discover a host of inner distractions and defenses from knowing what is in our hearts. We instinctively resist self-exposure. But if we persist in honest soul-searching, we will have the Spirit's help in pinpointing areas of unnoticed sin. Such conviction results in repentance —mourning for our waywardness and turning around. This process is what Joel called *rending the heart*.

> And rend your heart, and not your garments, and turn unto the Lord your God: for he is gracious and merciful, slow to anger, and of great kindness, and repenteth him of the evil.
>
> Joel 2:13

We are so skilled in self-deception that fasting may be necessary if we are to probe beyond our adjustments. Psychological defense mechanisms are very subtle; they do not announce their presence and they do prevent us from knowing how we really feel and what we honestly think. If we are earnestly seeking the rain of God's presence to reach us deeply, we must work at breaking up the fallow ground. Hear the words of Jeremiah:

> . . . Break up your fallow ground, and sow not among thorns. Circumcise yourselves to the Lord, and take away the foreskins of your heart, ye men of Judah and inhabitants of Jerusalem: lest my fury come forth like fire, and burn that none can quench it, because of the evil of your doings.
>
> Jeremiah 4:3, 4

Fasting clears away the thousand little things which quickly accumulate and clutter the heart and mind. It cuts through the corrosion, renewing our contact with God, in much the same way that batteries periodically need debris removed to restore their effectiveness.

The Old Testament terms *affliction of soul* and *humbling oneself* could be rendered in contemporary idiom as "taking off the mask." Removing the mask means more than dropping our pretense toward others; it means facing ourselves. To become receptive to God, we must stop trying to fool ourselves. He is a God of grace, but He is also a God of truth. We find both in Jesus Christ. We can receive His grace if we will deal with Him in terms of truth. It is in such times of utter honesty that God works His most profound changes upon our exposed areas. Paul said:

> But we all, with open face beholding as in a glass the glory of the Lord, are changed into the same image from glory to glory even as by the Spirit of the Lord.
>
> 2 Corinthians 3:18

This process of self-exposure is properly called *humbling oneself.*

## Motivation for Fasting

Motivation is simply that which moves us and makes us willing to do what we otherwise would not do. Few of us like to go without food, and fewer still enjoy facing their shortcomings and confessing sins. God often finds it necessary to prod us into self-exposure by allowing circumstances to crowd us until there is no other way out.

The Lord circumscribes us until we must cry for help. Our cry is specific because it grows out of the need at hand. But through the recognized need, God reaches to underlying problems we may never have been able to face. He probes beyond symptoms to the source. When God deals with us to effect deep, inner liberation, we are usually quite uncomfortable. Consequently, these times of spiritual surgery were described by graphic terms like *mourning* and *chastening*.

It is not unusual for God to motivate us through the need of loved ones. It is often easier for us to really cry to God for someone close to us than it seems to be for ourselves. But as we entreat God for others, He can reach us where *we* need it most as well.

Jesus told us in the Beatitudes that times of spiritual readjustment through chastening are good for us. He said we should be happy about them, at least in anticipation of their results.

> Blessed are they that mourn: for they shall be comforted.
>
> Matthew 5:4

The mourning Jesus is talking about is not self-pity. Self-pity is incapable of being comforted because it is its own satisfaction. Jesus is talking about real grief and sorrow, objective pain. Mourning is emotion tied to real life; it is caring and showing it. Fasting should be just as honest.

God responds to our determination to seek Him. He honors the honesty of those who confess by fasting and affliction of soul that their hearts need cleansing and change. God hears their cries.

Take, for example, Ezra and those accompanying him.

> Then I proclaimed a fast there, at the river of Ahava, that we might afflict ourselves before our God, to seek

of him a right way for us, and for our little ones, and
for all our substance. So we fasted and besought our
God for this: and he was intreated of us.

Ezra 8:21, 23

Why was this a time for Ezra and his company to fast? They
were motivated by need. They needed intervention which
could only come from God. The help they desired was clearly
God's will to provide, but they needed to make themselves
receptive. The issue was whether or not they would rely upon
natural means by asking for Babylonian soldiers. They knew
that they must commit themselves solely to God's keeping on
this dangerous journey. Through fasting they both purified
their own determination to trust God and strengthened their
own faith that He would see them through. Their focus was
set where it belonged.

## The Single Eye

Jesus taught that regular discipline in the realm of self-denial
will keep our focus right. So long as our goals coincide with
God's purposes, our eye is *single*—we steer a true course. But
if we allow our desires to wander and begin to set our affections
on gaining things for ourselves, that pure focus is clouded.

Our priorities determine our direction. If we are not making
steady progress toward God's goals for us, then we are being
distracted by other interests. Other things have become more
important to us than pleasing God. Our energies are being
invested in other channels.

For where your treasure is, there will your heart be also.
The light of the body is the eye: if therefore thine eye

be single, thy whole body shall be full of light. But if thine eye be evil, thy whole body shall be full of darkness. If therefore the light that is in thee be darkness, how great is that darkness! No man can serve two masters. . . . Ye cannot serve God and mammon.

Matthew 6:21-24

God is concerned with our focus because it determines our steering, our walk. Periodically, He calls for readjustment. He puts us into situations which will show us whether our hearts are set upon Him or intent upon pleasing ourselves. Is God central, or are things? What matters to us?

The Lord has told us that if we will judge ourselves, we will not need to be judged. Fasting is one means of judging ourselves as prevention of chastening. We can stop ourselves and let God search our hearts, without waiting for necessity. If we begin to feel cluttered and out of touch, we can ask God to show us why. We can follow the example of such men as Daniel or David, who learned to seek God early, before He became the only alternative. We can pray, with the added dimension of fasting:

Search me, O God, and know my heart: try me, and know my thoughts: And see if there be any wicked way in me, and lead me in the way everlasting.

Psalms 139:23, 24

If we are not able to hear independently, God may alert us to our need for repentance through His ministers. The Apostle James brought the Christians under his care to a stark realization of their need for repentance. He spared no words in letting

them know how God looked upon their condition. Division,
lust, worldliness—all these had provoked God's anger. But
worse yet, pride was causing God's grace to be turned away
from these people. It was time for them to humble themselves
and seek God's mercy.

> . . . . Wherefore he saith, God resisteth the proud, but
> giveth grace unto the humble. Submit yourselves there-
> fore to God. Resist the devil, and he will flee from you.
> Draw nigh to God, and he will draw nigh to you.
> Cleanse your hands, ye sinners; and purify your hearts,
> ye double minded.
>
>                                                    James 4:6-8

The two basic needs, according to James, were for them to
humble themselves and to restore or purify their focus. The
tone of James's exhortation resembles the Old Testament
prophets, especially as he continues with these words:

> Be afflicted, and mourn, and weep: let your laughter be
> turned to mourning, and your joy to heaviness. Humble
> yourselves in the sight of the Lord, and he shall lift you
> up.
>
>                                                   James 4:9, 10

## God Responds

When our fasting and mourning are born of genuine repentance, God responds. Even when He has already decreed punishment and set things in motion to bring it to pass, real
turning from sin will be rewarded. Fasting can be an effectual

means for making our turning wholehearted and for intensifying our call for mercy.

King Ahab and his wife Jezebel were wicked rulers of Israel. They used their authority to take advantage of their subjects. Not only did Ahab covet a vineyard which belonged to a man named Naboth, he and his wife plotted Naboth's death in order to take the vineyard. Fasting was used as part of the means for bringing about Naboth's murder. It was part of a deliberate trap of false accusation. The plot worked. The people stoned Naboth on the basis of the false witnesses' reports and Ahab gained the vineyard.

But the whole scheme did not escape the notice of God. He sent word to the prophet Elijah not only to expose this sin, but to decree judgment. The judgment was appropriately severe. In the very place Naboth died, the dogs would lick the blood of Ahab. His wife Jezebel, who devised the scheme to murder Naboth, would be eaten by dogs. The whole household would suffer judgment.

Ahab knew that he was found out. He also knew that the prophet's words had a ring of authority; they would indeed come to pass. He knew that God's decree of punishment was just, for he was guilty.

But Ahab also knew that God would respond to genuine repentance. He put all his energies into turning to God and demonstrating his sorrow for sin.

And it came to pass, when Ahab heard those words, that he rent his clothes, and put sackcloth upon his flesh, and fasted, and lay in sackcloth, and went softly.

1 Kings 21:27

He was not merely using the language of mourning, he was truly turning from sin. God was free to show mercy to Ahab. Because Ahab humbled himself, God's grace could flow to him.

> And the word of the Lord came to Elijah the Tishbite, saying, Seest thou how Ahab humbleth himself before me? because he humbleth himself before me, I will not bring the evil in his days: but in his son's days will I bring the evil upon his house.
>
> 1 Kings 21:28, 29

Surely there is a lesson in this story which will profit all of us! If repentance and fasting would make a difference in a case this extreme, we would all do well to heed God's warnings and come to Him by humbling ourselves whenever we become aware of our sinful ways.

# 7

# Fasting in Unity

One of the most common ways we allow sin to accumulate is on the corporate or group level. Every group—whether a local church or a nation—develops its own ways of doing things, its own norms or expectations. Individuals who are well adapted take great care to meet the standards set by group example, but these may not correspond to God's demands upon us as individuals or even meet His requirements for relationships.

Deviation from God's will is very subtle on the group level. Even when we examine ourselves, we often use as our point of reference the collective habits of the group. We check to make sure that we do not deviate too much from what is being done. The desire for social acceptability is strong; we all want to feel that we belong. But it is here that we often substitute social values for scriptural guidelines. We begin to follow relative standards instead of God's Word. The Apostle Paul said:

> For we dare not make ourselves of the number, or compare ourselves with some that commend themselves: but they measuring themselves by themselves . . . are not wise.
>
> 2 Corinthians 10:12

There is only one accurate plumb line; God measures His people. Our conformity must be to His Word. This was the message of most of the prophets. National standards and religious ideals had departed from their original adherence to God's Word; the nation as a whole had broken God's covenant.

## God Will Heal the Land

God had made provision for such national sin. He had established a warning signal to alert Israel to her need. He would send external calamity to call their attention back to God, if they failed to hear His voice through the prophets. He further had given directions to follow in the case of such emergencies.

> If I shut up heaven that there be no rain, or if I command the locusts to devour the land, or if I send pestilence among my people; If my people, which are called by my name, shall humble themselves, and pray, and seek my face, and turn from their wicked ways; then will I hear from heaven, and will forgive their sin, and will heal their land.
>
> 2 Chronicles 7:13, 14

These directions are fivefold. God requires:

1. His people must recognize their identity as His people; they must remember who they are. They are the special property of God, sealed by His name. They must again acknowledge His Lordship; the sense of belonging to God must supercede the claims of all other reference groups.

2. They must humble themselves—that is, they must fast and examine themselves before the Lord. They cannot continue deceiving themselves about their inner life. Sin must be faced. Pride must be abased.

3. They must pray. Their requests must be made known to God by verbal petition. Carrying concern and burden on the inside will not suffice; they must ask God's intervention. Aimless anxiety—the cause of worry and depression—will be released only as specific petitions are directed to God in faith.

4. They are to seek—earnestly seek—the restoration of God's favor. If His face shines upon them, peace will be theirs. His personal approval must become all-important as the only measure of conduct. This approval is manifest by His presence in glory.

5. They must turn, repent, change their ways. Those who claim His name must depart from their familiar sin. Repentance is never real unless it changes our behavior. Tears, pious words, and religious ceremonies never suffice; moral decisions must be made and carried out. Godly repentance is never limited to thoughts and emotions; God makes lasting changes in our character.

When these conditions are met, God will do His part. First, He will hear the petitions. He will accept the prayers. Second, He will forgive all the sins that have been confessed. He will cover in mercy all that was exposed to Him. Third, He will heal the land. The chastening can be removed because His people have heeded His call. They can again enjoy national protection and favor because His Lordship has been reestablished.

## The Formula Works

Did this formula for meeting national emergency work? Did the nation of Israel ever test it? Yes, they did. Not many years after Solomon had recorded these directions, they were put to the test during a time of war. Jehoshaphat had unwisely entangled Judah in an alliance with an ungodly king. God was angry, but in faithfulness He sent a prophet to warn Jehoshaphat.

> And Jehu the son of Hanani the seer went out to meet him, and said to king Jehoshaphat, Shouldest thou help the ungodly, and love them that hate the Lord? therefore is wrath upon thee from before the Lord.
>
> 2 Chronicles 19:2

On the heels of the prophetic word came the set alarm—national calamity! They were militarily overwhelmed.

> And Jehoshaphat feared, and set himself to seek the Lord, and proclaimed a fast throughout all Judah. And Judah gathered themselves together, to ask help of the Lord: even out of all the cities of Judah they came to seek the Lord.
>
> 2 Chronicles 20:3, 4

It was not enough for the leaders to repent and to pray; the whole nation must fast, pray, and seek the Lord. The people could not sit back and criticize their government and expect God's intervention; they must involve themselves in the plight of the nation.

Jehoshaphat led in prayer and directed attention back to the basis for expecting intervention—God's promise. Faith grew as they reminded themselves of God's steadfast word.

> If, when evil cometh upon us, as the sword, judgment, or pestilence, or famine, we stand before this house, and in thy presence (for thy name is in this house,) and cry unto thee in our affliction, then thou wilt hear and help.
>
> 2 Chronicles 20:9

In the context of fulfilling God's requirements, they made their specific request known. God heard and acted. He assumed full responsibility for the battle.

## Fasting for Unity of Focus

A similar instance of national involvement occurred much earlier in Israel's history, even before these directions and promises had been given to Solomon. Nevertheless the same principle operated. God was using the distress to draw the people together in seeking His aid.

The occasion was the civil war between the nation of Israel and the seceding tribe of Benjamin. The tribe of Benjamin was prevailing against Israel, even though they were greatly outnumbered.

Twice the leaders of Israel sought advice from God, the second time even with weeping. But both times the guidance was inadequate. Something more was needed. How could they receive clear, reliable direction? The dimension of fasting was added—united fasting and prayer.

Then all the children of Israel, and all the people, went up, and came unto the house of God, and wept, and sat there before the Lord, and fasted that day until even, and offered burnt offerings and peace offerings before the Lord.

Judges 20:26

Then again they inquired of the Lord for direction.

And Phinehas, the son of Eleazar, the son of Aaron, stood before [the ark of God's presence] . . . saying, Shall I yet again go out to battle against the children of Benjamin my brother, or shall I cease?

Judges 20:28

God was pleased with their corporate openness and readiness to obey. His answer was prompt and specific.

. . . And the Lord said, Go up; for tomorrow I will deliver them into thine hand.

Judges 20:28

The leaders could receive clear direction because prayer and fasting on the part of all the people was behind them. They were truly representing the whole people because prayer and fasting had brought about a unity of involvement.

Many people criticize the idea of a corporate fast, especially if any public prayer is involved. They claim that it is only show and that God could not honor such a practice. Yet we find examples of public, corporate crying to God throughout Scripture. And it is there for a reason: God purposes to create a depth of unity in corporate concern that cannot come about in any other way.

So long as we go our separate ways—tending our own jobs, fulfilling our own schedules, eating at separate tables, it is hard to really pray together for a joint concern. But fasting, not only from food, but from all other clutter, frees the attention of all to converge upon a shared concern. Total involvement in seeking God's intervention is now possible as a group—whether a local church, a city, or a nation. Answers to prayer are released in a greater dimension because of the unity in caring enough to cease from selfish interests and come together as one to find God's help. Did the psalmist not promise a special blessing to those united before God?

> Behold, how good and how pleasant it is for brethren to dwell together in unity! It is like the precious ointment upon the head, that ran down upon the beard, even Aaron's beard: that went down to the skirts of his garments; As the dew of Hermon, and as the dew that descended upon the mountains of Zion: for there the Lord commanded the blessing, even life for evermore.
>
> Psalms 133

The anointing breaks yokes and brings results anytime, but the corporate anointing received through unity in prayer and fasting removes even stubborn and resistant roadblocks to health, direction or progress. Its power is that of collective focus and group openness before God. When each individual member cares enough to set aside his own interests for the sake of the group concern, how greatly the focus is magnified!

## Spiritual Leadership Is Needed

One important difference between Bible days and now must be pointed out: in those days of theocracy, national leaders were also the spiritual leaders. There was no separation of church and state as there is today. Then it was natural for the king to lead the people back to God. Now the responsibility for spiritual leadership rests upon leaders in the church. Respected ministers among God's people will have to recognize God's call and determine when corporate fasting is necessary.

When the land is being made desolate through chastening, our spiritual leaders must interpret God's dealings and direct His people in response. The prophet Joel said:

> Gird yourselves, and lament, ye priests: howl, ye ministers of the altar: come, lie all night in sackcloth, ye ministers of my God: for the meat offering and the drink offering is withholden from the house of your God. Sanctify ye a fast, call a solemn assembly, gather the elders and all the inhabitants of the land into the house of the Lord your God, and cry unto the Lord.
>
> Joel 1:13, 14

Spiritual leadership is first one of example, and then one of direction. After the ministers have applied the word to themselves, they can involve their people until all share in the experience of corporate repentance.

The leaders must hear God's direction and follow it before it can be passed on with authority. We see this principle illustrated in the leadership of Nehemiah. He first heard of the distress of God's people in Jerusalem and began to entreat God for them. The burden increased as he became more aware of the need. He took it to God. He cared enough to act.

> And it came to pass, when I heard these words, that I sat down and wept, and mourned certain days, and fasted, and prayed before the God of heaven.
>
> Nehemiah 1:4

Because Nehemiah cared enough to invest himself in prayer and fasting, God put practical means into his hands. Nehemiah was set in a position of influence. His example could affect others.

Later on, in the process of restoring the walls of Jerusalem, Nehemiah was able to involve the entire remnant in a similar prayer and fast unto God. Nehemiah could bring them into the experience he himself possessed. Because he cared, it could become contagious.

> Now in the twenty and fourth day of this month the children of Israel were assembled with fasting, and with sackcloths, and earth upon them. And the seed of Israel separated themselves from all strangers, and stood and confessed their sins, and the iniquities of their fathers. And they stood up in their place, and read in the book of the law of the Lord their God one fourth part of the day; and another fourth part they confessed, and worshipped the Lord their God.
>
> Nehemiah 9:1-3

Most of us have reacted against the church's arbitrary setting of calendars. We see little profit in fast days mechanically obeyed because they are part of an annual observance. But in protesting this, we have erred to the opposite extreme in failing to see the importance of leadership in directing corporate response to God during times of local or national chastening.

Who is to interpret the signs of the times responsibly if not those who have learned through years of discipline how to recognize the Word of the Lord? Who has the authority to lead multitudes but the man God has initiated through personal experience? Who can relate prophecy to contemporary concerns but the man who has not only studied God's Word, but learned His ways?

Hear again the call of the prophet Joel:

> Blow the trumpet in Zion, sanctify a fast, call a solemn assembly: Gather the people, sanctify the congregation, assemble the elders, gather the children, and those that suck the breasts: let the bridegroom go forth of his chamber, and the bride out of her closet. Let the priests, the ministers of the Lord, weep between the porch and the altar, and let them say, Spare thy people, O Lord, and give not thine heritage to reproach, that the heathen should rule over them: wherefore should they say among the people, Where is their God?
>
> Joel 2:15-17

A time of corporate fasting will upset everybody; social plans will be set aside, family life disrupted. Before undertaking such a large-scale upheaval, the leaders themselves must be sure.

They do not carelessly ask such a sacrifice. But once they themselves have given full heed to the Word of the Lord, they can ask the people for total commitment with confidence. They know that God will honor this action. All can enter into this time of intense focus upon God with full assurance that God will in turn focus upon them.

> Then will the Lord be jealous for his land, and pity his people. Yea, the Lord will answer and say unto his people, Behold, I will send you corn, and wine, and oil, and ye shall be satisfied therewith: and I will no more make you a reproach among the heathen.
>
> Joel 2:18, 19

We must wholeheartedly follow our leaders when they are directed to call for corporate repentance and supplication, but we cannot confuse corporate obedience with personal responsibility. There are many times when God calls us aside personally to break up our fallow ground by fasting, and there are exceptional occasions when change can come only through group upheaval and united focus.

# 8

# Fasting Is Ministry

Focus upon God of necessity begins with cleansing, but it certainly does not stop there. The blood is applied to give us access into God's very presence. The blood of Jesus takes away sin—even the memory of it—to clear the way for fellowship and service. The Hebrews' writer said:

> How much more shall the blood of Christ, who through the eternal Spirit offered himself without spot to God, purge your conscience from dead works to serve the living God?
>
> Hebrews 9:14

Once we are personally clean before the Lord, we can serve Him acceptably and minister to others. But occasions for prayer and fasting continue; they have a different purpose.

Ministry requires preparation, a progressive separation unto God. This is accomplished through providential chastening and personal discipline. Fasting plays a definite part.

Since Old Testament times, fasting has been recognized as one means of separating ourselves. The Nazarite vow included limited fasting.

> Speak unto the children of Israel, and say unto them,
> When either man or woman shall separate themselves
> to vow a vow of a Nazarite, to separate themselves unto
> the Lord: He shall . . . drink no vinegar of wine, or
> vinegar of strong drink, neither shall he drink any liquor
> of grapes, nor eat moist grapes, or dried. All the days
> of his separation shall he eat nothing that is made of
> the vine tree, from the kernels even to the husk.
>
> Numbers 6:2-4

A similar separation was prophesied of John the Baptist even before his birth. The angel Gabriel told Zacharias concerning John:

> For he shall be great in the sight of the Lord, and shall
> drink neither wine nor strong drink; and he shall be
> filled with the Holy Ghost, even from his mother's
> womb.
>
> Luke 1:15

In actuality, John's diet was even more restricted. His focus upon God demanded complete separation from the society of his day; he prepared himself in the desert. There his food consisted of locusts (the nut of the tree) and wild honey (*see* Matthew 3:1-4). He lived in great simplicity to allow maximum freedom to concentrate upon God.

Fasting is a part of preparation for ministry because it is discipline in the area of self-denial. Involvement with the needs of others—and that is what ministry is all about—costs us many conveniences and preferences. We must be able to deny ourselves to put the needs of others first. We must have the resourcefulness of being able to reorder our priorities according to the situation. We must know that we are in control of our own bodies and of time. We can then count on ourselves to be able to give what is needed in ministry. The Apostle Paul described the disciplined life in military terms. He said to Timothy:

> Thou therefore endure hardness, as a good soldier of Jesus Christ. No man that warreth entangleth himself with the affairs of this life; that he may please him who hath chosen him to be a soldier.
>
> 2 Timothy 2:3, 4

Uriah the Hittite was a seasoned warrior in David's army. He knew that alertness required freedom from the clutter of any other involvements during the time of battle. He tried to resist the enticements of King David to lull him into carelessness. This natural scene pictures spiritual realities as well.

> And Uriah said unto David, The ark, and Israel, and Judah, abide in tents; and my lord Joab, and the servants of my lord, are encamped in the open fields; shall I then go into mine house, to eat and to drink, and to lie with my wife? as thou livest, and as thy soul liveth, I will not do this thing.
>
> 2 Samuel 11:11

The Apostle Paul had learned that ministry requires complete flexibility to adjust to any situation in the Lord. He had learned the ordering of his priorities by many years' choices to put the Lord and His work first. When necessity demanded deprivation, he was equal to it.

> But in all things approving ourselves as the ministers of God, in much patience, in afflictions, in necessities, in distresses, In stripes, in imprisonments, in tumults, in labours, in watchings, in fastings.
>
> 2 Corinthians 6:4, 5

> Are they ministers of Christ? I am more; in labours more abundant, in stripes above measure, in prisons more frequent, in deaths oft. . . . In weariness and painfulness, in watchings often, in hunger and thirst, in fastings often, in cold and nakedness.
>
> 2 Corinthians 11:23, 27

## Fasting Is Worship

Our first ministry is to God; it is the presenting of ourselves as a living sacrifice. Presenting our bodies in obedient worship is a means for bringing our soul into harmony with God. Fasting is one of several means God has made available for the physical expression of obedience. It is one way we can deliberately present our bodies in the service of God.

The Apostle Paul recognized the principle of communicating spiritual choices to ourselves by means of bodily obedience when he described our reasonable service of worship.

> I beseech you therefore, brethren, by the mercies of God, that ye present your bodies a living sacrifice, holy,

acceptable unto God, which is your reasonable service.
. . . that ye may prove what is that good, and acceptable, and perfect will of God.

Romans 12:1, 2

Fasting puts our soul in right perspective, in balance with
our spirit and body, so that we can worship in spirit and in truth
in greater dimension. It is one way of communicating to our
own souls, "You can't fill up everything; God has a higher
priority."

Hunger in this affluent society is more often the habit of our
souls than the body's cry for nourishment. Much eating is only
habit. We often eat when we are not truly in need of food and
when we would do better not to eat. Eating is more often tied
to social and emotional needs than to physical ones. Consequently, fasting is more a discipline of the soul than of the
body.

Fasting serves to make us stop dissipating our attention and
return to focus on God. It calls a halt to our scattered activities
and restores perspective. Basic to all our activity is relationship
with God. But it is very easy to get off-center and be carried
away onto tangents. Fasting pulls us up short. We can reset our
focus.

Worship serves many purposes, but one which we often
overlook is the benefit it gives to us in restoring right perspective and balance. Through worship we magnify God. We deliberately choose and confess that He is larger and more important than all else that concerns us. We magnify Him with our
praises, our songs, our acts of obedience, and most of all by
giving Him our attention. In order to magnify God, we must

minimize our problems and selfish interests. We do not minimize ourselves, because as we become the vehicles of total worship, we are fulfilled. We become what God made us to be. But we do minimize the petty grievances, the self-preoccupation, and the cares of this life that too easily clutter our soul.

Fasting is a prayer against clutter. In the physical realm our bodies are cleansed during periods of fasting. Impurities are purged from our system. Excess fat is burned. But in our souls, too, clutter and excess is removed as our attention is taken from everything but the Lord. As our soul thus magnifies the Lord, our spirits are freed to rejoice in God.

The early church considered fasting a very definite part of ministering to the Lord. They did not fast in order to hear direction from the Lord, as so many claim; they fasted as part of their ministry of worship. They considered it a part of their reasonable service. God in turn honored their praise and worship with His presence and Word.

> As they ministered to the Lord, and fasted, the Holy Ghost said, Separate me Barnabas and Saul for the work whereunto I have called them. And when they had fasted and prayed, and laid their hands on them, they sent them away.
>
> Acts 13:2, 3

During their worship, they received so much of the presence of God that they had to share the overflow. They began to lay hands on Barnabas and Saul to impart that extra life they had received. Worship came first and ministry to others came as the result of the overflow of His Spirit.

Why was fasting a part of this worship? It was part of the self-forgetfulness which is basic to ministering unto the Lord and to others. We must become preoccupied with the Lord Himself and then with His concerns to truly minister unto Him. If we are still taken up with our own concerns, we have nothing to give.

Basic to all worship is the element of sacrifice. Sacrifice in its simplest terms means giving up something which matters to us; it is giving up our own desires in order to please another.

King David communicated the essence of sacrifice in his decision to pay for land to offer burnt offerings. Araunah had offered him the use of the land without cost, but David knew that the cost validated the worship.

> And the king [David] said unto Araunah, Nay; but I will surely buy it of thee at a price: neither will I offer burnt offerings unto the Lord my God of that which doth cost me nothing. So David bought the threshing-floor and the oxen for fifty shekels of silver. And David built there an altar unto the Lord, and offered burnt offerings and peace offerings. So the Lord was intreated for the land, and the plague was stayed from Israel.
>
> 2 Samuel 24:24, 25

We must be careful not to confuse the necessary ingredient of cost to ourselves with the idea of meriting or buying something from God. God does not need our sacrifices or our fasting—we do. We need the ability to deny ourselves in order to give to God.

## Caring for Others

All ministry is giving. First, we present ourselves to God and then we give to Him and to others that which He has freely given to us. We mentioned earlier the trilogy of service and the balance which God desires. Without almsgiving (in its expanded sense), prayer and fasting tend toward self-centeredness. God has designed us to grow in love toward Him in proportion to our love toward others to prevent our becoming introspective and preoccupied. The Apostle John stressed the interrelatedness of love for God and for others this way:

> If a man say, I love God, and hateth his brother, he is a liar: for he that loveth not his brother whom he hath seen, how can he love God whom he hath not seen? And this commandment have we from him, That he who loveth God love his brother also.
>
> 1 John 4:20, 21

Fasting, we have said, is focus upon God. How can we ever combine focus upon God and caring for others? Are these not competitive? No, they are complementary. God has provided a way for us to fast for others, to seek Him intently for their needs. In such intercession the key is identification. We put ourselves in the place of others before God.

At this point, we must remember that basic to fasting is humbling ourselves. In no way can we intercede effectively for others if we lift ourselves above them in our own minds. If we judge others, we lose all power to pray for them. Faith only works by love and love covers the multitude of sins.

A good illustration of fasting as intercession, by identification with the needs of others, is that of Ezra.

Ezra, like Nehemiah and Zechariah, was concerned with the restoration of Jerusalem after the long Babylonian captivity. In spite of exemplary leadership, the returned exiles soon forgot their identity as the people of God. It was no longer important to them that they belonged to God. Instead, they freely mixed with the strangers who had inhabited the land in their absence. They intermingled against the clear command of God. By neglecting separation unto God, they were rapidly forfeiting His favor and help (*see* Ezra 9:1,2).

What did Ezra do? Did he immediately condemn them to destruction? Did he find a soapbox and righteously proclaim God's just judgment was soon to come upon them as they deserved? No. He fasted. He took it all to heart.

He did not fast for his own need alone; he fasted for them. Certainly he asked for wisdom and direction, but his prayer and fasting did not end there. Apparently part of God's direction was to continue in fasting and prayer as intercession. He was to put himself in the position of those who had sinned but lacked ability to pray for themselves. He was to react totally as they should have reacted. They should have repented in sackcloth and ashes had they been in the position to hear what God was saying. This Ezra did for them.

> And when I heard this thing, I rent my garment and
> my mantle, and plucked off the hair of my head and of
> my beard, and sat down astonied.
>
> Ezra 9:3

A few intercessors joined him. This small group of intercessors identified themselves with the whole remnant who had sinned. They prayed as representatives for all the people. Ezra led in the prayer of identification:

> And at the evening sacrifice I arose up from my heaviness; and having rent my garment and my mantle, I fell upon my knees, and spread out my hands unto the Lord my God. And said, O my God, I am ashamed and blush to lift up my face to thee, my God: for our iniquities are increased over our head, and our trespass is grown up unto the heavens.
>
> Ezra 9:5, 6

Here we find the two essential elements of effective intercession: identification with God *(O my God)* and identification with the needy *(our iniquities)*. Since Ezra was entreating God as if he were in their position of needing repentance, he used behavior provided to express affliction of soul: rending his garments, shaving his head and beard, kneeling, and fasting.

> Then Ezra rose up from before the house of God, and went into the chamber of Johanan the son of Eliashib: and when he came thither, he did eat no bread, nor drink water: for he mourned because of the transgression of them that had been carried away.
>
> Ezra 10:6

After fully identifying himself with the people's sin, he could lead them to repentance without pride or arrogance on his part. His focus upon God had not elevated his opinion of himself, making him unusable. It had made him more aware that temptation and sin are common to man. His double identification, with God and with the people, had caused him to share the feelings of both. He could now communicate honestly, from the heart, to God for the people and to the people for God. The people felt the strength of his involvement and responded.

> And Ezra the priest stood up, and said unto them, Ye have transgressed, and have taken strange wives, to increase the trespass of Israel. Now therefore make confession unto the Lord God of your fathers, and do his pleasure: and separate yourselves from the people of the land, and from the strange wives. Then all the congregation answered and said with a loud voice, As thou hast said, so must we do.
>
> Ezra 10:10-12

How many ministers who desire the power to move people are willing to follow Ezra's example of identification? Most of us like to think of intercession as praying for someone from our superior vantage point. It is hard for us to see ourselves as one with those who have problems. Nevertheless, this depth of identification is expected of all of us who belong to the body of Christ. Our caring must go that far. Paul exhorted:

> That there should be no schism in the body; but that the members should have the same care one for another. And whether one member suffer, all the members suffer with it. . . .
>
> 1 Corinthians 12:25, 26

Similar intercession was made by Daniel when he discovered by reading Jeremiah's writings that it was time for God to restore His people. He made his voice, his heart, and his body the vehicle for the prayer that all those in captivity should have been praying for themselves. He acted as their representative by identification, and this included fasting.

> And I set my face unto the Lord God, to seek by prayer and supplications, with fasting, and sackcloth, and ashes: And I prayed unto the Lord my God, and made my confession, and said, O Lord, the great and dreadful God, keeping the covenant and mercy to them that love him and to them that keep his commandments; We have sinned, and have committed iniquity, and have done wickedly, and have rebelled, even by departing from thy precepts and from thy judgments: Neither have we hearkened unto thy servants the prophets, which spake in thy name to our kings, our princes, and our fathers, and to all the people of the land.

> Daniel 9:3-6

Wait a minute! Didn't Daniel begin this time of seeking God because he had heard something in the prophecies of Jeremiah? What does he mean, *neither have we hearkened unto thy servants the prophets?* Daniel had sacrificed his own position of righteousness in order to become one with the whole nation who had not listened. His prayer could have no power if he held himself aloof from the people for whom he was praying.

Because Daniel confessed identity with the sinning people, he had faith to ask God to do the same.

O Lord, hear; O Lord, forgive; O Lord, hearken and do;
defer not, for thine own sake, O my God: for the city
and thy people are called by thy name.

Daniel 9:19

Daniel held on to God with one hand and to the people with
the other. He would not deny his identification with either.
From this position, his prayer and fasting prevailed. This was
ministry both to God and to the people—the ministry of reconciliation.

Jesus Christ left His atonement as the supreme example of
intercession for reconciliation between God and man. We are
exhorted to share His mind.

Let nothing be done through strife or vainglory; but in
lowliness of mind let each esteem other better than
themselves. Look not every man on his own things, but
every man on the things of others. Let this mind be in
you, which was also in Christ Jesus: Who, being in the
form of God, thought it not robbery to be equal with
God: But made himself of no reputation, and took
upon him the form of a servant, and was made in the
likeness of men: And being found in fashion as a man,
he humbled himself, and became obedient unto death,
even the death of the cross.

Philippians 2:3-8

Fasting—self-denial of any kind—is so little to ask us to do
for our brother, in light of all Jesus has done for us.

# 9

# Fasting at God's Initiative

Fruitfulness in any undertaking depends upon our source of authority. Jesus was effective in creative ministry because He did and said only what was given to Him by His Father. He was sent not to do His own will, but His Father's. His obedience gave Him authority.

The success of His disciples depended upon the passing on of this authority. When they went forth as sent men to obey specific orders, the strongholds of the enemy were shaken. Even demons were subject to their word.

This principle was demonstrated in Peter's personal experience where he would understand it best—in his business. Peter thought he really knew his field. He was an experienced fisherman. But Jesus had something new to teach him—the initiative of God makes all the difference.

Peter and those working with him had tried all night, using the best methods they knew. These were veteran fishermen and they knew plenty. But nothing worked. Then Jesus, who obviously had little experience with boats or fishing, had the audacity to tell them to go out into deep waters and put down their nets for a large catch. Anyone knew you could not catch fish in nets in deep water. Besides, they had exhausted every possible spot the night before. There just weren't any fish to be had at this time.

But Peter knew Jesus well enough to obey His word and at least try it, even if it did sound ridiculous. He had seen Jesus heal his mother and cast out demons from many sick people. Perhaps He could make a difference in this situation too. Luke tells the story this way:

> Now when [Jesus] had left speaking, he said unto Simon, Launch out into the deep, and let down your nets for a draught. And Simon answering said unto him, Master, we have toiled all the night, and have taken nothing: nevertheless at thy word I will let down the net. And when they had this done, they inclosed a great multitude of fishes: and their net brake. And they beckoned unto their partners, which were in the other ship, that they should come and help them. And they came, and filled both the ships, so that they began to sink.
>
> Luke 5:4-7

Peter's reaction reveals that he was learning the lesson. He responded to Jesus' authority. He confessed his submission to Jesus' Lordship. Now he was ready to be commissioned by that same authority to fish for men. His success in ministry would depend upon Jesus' initiative, just as it had in fishing.

## Fasting and Authority

Fasting is no exception to Kingdom principles. It is subject to the same rules that govern prayer, almsgiving, and ministry. Fasting is not something we do in order to manipulate God. We cannot put, as it were, a wrestling hold upon Him by our long and severe abstinence. Fasting is only effective when it is done in response to God's initiative.

A striking illustration of such initiative and response is found in the Book of Jonah. The story was as follows. A heathen city was suddenly alerted to repentance by the warning of impending judgment through the Hebrew prophet, Jonah. His message apparently thundered with such authority that the people trembled to the core at the sound of each word. Their reaction was profound.

Beginning with the king himself, the city of Nineveh set about to fast and mourn for their sin and to cry to God for mercy. The king's example lent authority to his decree. Cooperation was forthcoming on every level.

> So the people of Nineveh believed God, and proclaimed a fast, and put on sackcloth, from the greatest of them even to the least of them. For word came unto the king of Nineveh, and he arose from his throne, and he laid his robe from him, and covered him with sackcloth, and sat in ashes. And he caused it to be proclaimed and published through Nineveh by the decree of the king and his nobles, saying, Let neither man nor beast, herd nor flock, taste any thing: let them not feed, nor drink water: But let man and beast be covered with sackcloth, and cry mightily unto God: yea, let them turn every one from his evil way, and from the violence that is in their hands.
>
> Jonah 3:5-8

Both faith to heed God's warning and repentance from their exposed sin were granted by God. He had sent His Word.

Because they heard, they could respond by turning away from themselves and their wicked ways to God. So drastic was the needed change that fasting was spontaneous.

Expectation was born of the deep sense of God's initiation. They were not fasting just to be doing something. Fasting and repentance arose from the urgency of the day. God alone could avert total destruction, if He could be prevailed upon to change His mind.

Warnings from God always engender hope as well as fear. They create fear sufficient to motivate repentance, but kindle hope that supplication may avail.

> Who can tell if God will turn and repent, and turn away from his fierce anger, that we perish not? And God saw their works, that they turned from their evil way; and God repented of the evil, that he had said that he would do unto them; and he did it not.
>
> Jonah 3:9, 10

Because Nineveh fasted in response to God's initiative, it was effective. Their focus was restored and God heard their supplications for mercy.

## Focus Intensifies Authority

Fasting increases our awareness of God's initiative, and consequently intensifies our authority in prayer and ministry. Some have thought that fasting impressed God and thereby induced Him to share more of His power, but not so. Rather, as we set aside the many other sources of direction, it is easier for us to distinguish the leading of the Lord. The problem is not with God's speaking, but with our hearing. We must turn aside from the clamor and really listen.

Fasting in itself is not the power, God is. But when our hearts are freed from debris and clutter, the Holy Spirit can once again flow through us freely. We are restored to usefulness as His channels.

Faith is a natural response to hearing God's Word and seeing His face in clear focus. Uncluttering the heart so that focus upon God is again possible is therefore a means for recovering faith. Faith always comes by hearing, but our hearing is greatly improved when we take time to be honest with ourselves before God.

Our awareness of authority is usually diminished because we become involved with too many activities. We dissipate our energies and attention in so many directions that we lose our focus. Loss of focus is reflected in our experience as unsureness and indecisiveness. Before long, we are involved in undertakings which God did not assign. We thought we could help. We felt that we had a good idea. But God's initiative was not behind us and we found ourselves bewildered by seeming ineffectiveness even in ministries in which God previously used us.

Such was the case with Jesus' disciples. They had been commissioned by Jesus not only to preach, but to heal the sick, cast out demons, and even raise the dead. They had experienced no small measure of success. But in the clutter of their activity in ministry their focus had become dimmed. They were not hearing as often and as clearly, and their faith waned.

At that moment a need arose which was beyond ordinary demands. Extra resources were needed. A man brought his lunatic son for deliverance, and it was clearly a case of demon possession. They tried their usual techniques, but there was no authority.

Jesus, in the meantime, had taken Peter, James, and John apart with Him to a mountaintop for a time of intense prayer and encounter with God. Very probably, they fasted as well. It was at this time that Jesus was transfigured before them and that Moses and Elijah conversed with Jesus (*see* Matthew 17:1-3). The voice of the Father was heard with fresh authority:

> ... This is my beloved Son, in whom I am well pleased, hear ye him. And when the disciples heard it, they fell on their face, and were sore afraid.
>
> Matthew 17:5, 6

After this time of focus upon God, Jesus and the three disciples with Him were charged with a renewed sense of mission and authority. They were ready for the situation confronting the other disciples.

When they came to the scene of activity, the man rehearsed his story for Jesus. The powerlessness of the disciples had increased the man's desperation and doubt. But Jesus calmly took command of the situation.

> And Jesus rebuked the devil; and he departed out of him: and the child was cured from that very hour. Then came the disciples to Jesus apart, and said, Why could not we cast him out? And Jesus said unto them, Because of your unbelief: for verily I say unto you, If ye have faith as a grain of mustard seed, ye shall say unto

this mountain, Remove hence to yonder place; and it shall remove; and nothing shall be impossible unto you. Howbeit this kind goeth not out but by prayer and fasting.

Matthew 17:18-21

Unbelief is often a problem of focus. The need looms larger than God when we look at it. Awareness of God can be crowded by other thoughts. Such difficulties with thought-life are part of our daily battle in overcoming temptation and walking by faith.

Seasons of temptation come to all of us. They are times of heaviness and distraction. Problems surround us on all sides; we seem unable to surmount them. Concentration is harassed by pressing concerns. Even our times of prayer become a hassle with our own thoughts. At these times, we may recognize that we are dealing with more than ourselves; there is a warfare and our weak places are being assaulted.

The scene of spiritual warfare is most often the imagination. There the battle rages in the form of disturbing thoughts until we find resources in God to restore control.

For though we walk in the flesh, we do not war after the flesh: (For the weapons of our warfare are not carnal, but mighty through God to the pulling down of strong holds;) Casting down imaginations, and every high thing that exalteth itself against the knowledge of God, and bringing into captivity every thought to the obedience of Christ.

2 Corinthians 10:3-5

Notice that it is the high things which need to be brought under control. We all have a tendency to think too highly of ourselves and to exaggerate the importance of our own affairs. These tendencies are played upon during times of warfare. We are tempted to make our own solutions and to show the world who we are. Such were the temptations of Jesus which He overcame during His forty-day wilderness fast.

How did fasting help Jesus overcome these suggestions? It provided a way for Him to readjust His focus and to sort out His thoughts. By focusing only upon God, He eliminated the pull of all other thoughts. He deliberately abstained from any other reliance or even any other words than God's. He refused to allow His mind to run in its own way, but channeled it by deliberate choice.

Centuries before, the prophet Isaiah had linked mental discipline with fasting. Fasting, according to Isaiah and the other prophets, was a turning of the whole person away from self-centered routine and habit to a fresh encounter with God. It was a deliberate disruption to enhance new insight and bypass habitual hang-ups. Isaiah's words were:

> If thou turn away thy foot from the sabbath, from doing thy pleasure on my holy day; and call the sabbath a delight, the holy of the Lord, honourable; and shalt honour him, not doing thine own ways, nor finding thine own pleasure, nor speaking thine own words.
>
> Isaiah 58:13

Isaiah was telling the people of his day to welcome the fasts God had appointed. The rest which God wanted to give included release from our own thoughts.

When ordinary discipline fails to keep our thoughts in check, extraordinary measures may be needed. Fasting may be in order. This is particularly so if the turn our thinking takes is negative and unbelieving. We need a restoration of focus upon God, His goodness, and mercy.

Fasting was never meant to be a substitute for regular self-discipline. Rather, it is an intensification of self-discipline during times of special need.

Bible scholar D. Martyn Lloyd-Jones succinctly related fasting to daily discipline with these words:

You should always keep under the body, but that does not mean you should always fast. Fasting is something unusual or exceptional . . . while discipline should be perpetual and permanent. I therefore cannot accept such texts as "I keep under my body," and "mortify your members that are upon the earth," as being a part of fasting. In other words, moderation in eating is a very good way of keeping the body under, but that is not fasting.

Failure to understand the difference between normal self-denial which enables us to show moderation in all things, and fasting which is an exceptional time of intense focus upon God, leads to extremism instead of balance. For example, some people struggle with self-indulgence to the point of gluttony week after week. Then they expect a long fast to eliminate the accumulated excess from their bodies and to cure their insatiable desire for food. Often these people return to their eating with intensified vigor once the fast is over. More often, they find that their muscles of self-discipline are so little developed that they are unable to fast successfully.

## A Fast That Failed

There is a fast recorded in Scripture that proved a total failure. It was not initiated by God, but by the people themselves. They had divorced the outward abstinence from inner change. God can only change us if we are willing to change.

Neither prayer nor fasting will compensate for repentance. It is meant to prepare the way for it. Leaders can set an example and even make the way by intercession, but the people must follow. They must return to God for themselves.

During a time of drought, Jeremiah entreated God for the people. National calamity had come as judgment upon national sin. But they had walked so long in their own ways that repentance was no longer an available response. They had refused to hear for so long that they no longer could hear—and we must hear in order to turn. It was no longer a time for prayer and fasting; judgment was set.

> Then said the Lord unto me [Jeremiah], Pray not for this people for their good. When they fast, I will not hear their cry; and when they offer burnt offering and an oblation, I will not accept them: but I will consume them by the sword, and by the famine, and by the pestilence.
>
> Jeremiah 14:11, 12

Fasting serves to unclutter our hearts before God; to make openness available even in the deep places. But what good is this if we have basically set our will against God? Exposure could only reveal deep-seated sin.

During the reign of Jehoiakim, one of the last kings of Judah before the captivity, the people literally rejected God's Word during a time of fasting. Jeremiah sent Baruch to read a message from God to the leaders and people of Judah. The roll contained hard words, an exposure of their collective sins since the last national revival. But had they hearkened, they could have been spared. God had said through Jeremiah:

> Take thee a roll of a book, and write therein all the words that I have spoken unto thee against Israel, and against Judah, and against all the nations, from the day I spake unto thee, from the days of Josiah, even unto this day. It may be that the house of Judah will hear all the evil which I purpose to do unto them; that they may return every man from his evil way: that I may forgive their iniquity and their sin.

> Jeremiah 36:2, 3

Baruch took the roll to read to the people during their time of fasting according to Jeremiah's instructions. The time of fasting should have been their time of maximum openness and tenderness before the Lord. They were to rend their hearts and make room for His reproof. Their attention was optimal; they had set aside their distracting duties to focus upon God. What better time to hear and to profit?

But such was not the case. The fast was called, and the people came in response to the king's proclamation. But their hearts had strayed so far that they were no longer within earshot of God—even during a period of fasting! The reading of God's message only kindled their anger against God's messengers. They even dared to burn the words of the Lord in total contempt for His warning.

And it came to pass, that when Jehudi had read three or four leaves, he cut it with the penknife, and cast it into the fire that was on the hearth, until all the roll was consumed in the fire. . . . Yet they were not afraid, nor rent their garments, neither the king, nor any of his servants that heard all these words.

Jeremiah 36:23, 24

Their hearts had been hardened beyond the point of response. Fasting was of no avail because they were rejecting God. God had no alternative left but that of judgment.

# 10

# The Fast Chosen by God

God has not left us to speculate about fasting—His directions are specific. He has clearly told us what to avoid and what our aim should be. The prophet Isaiah in particular uncovered God's heart-attitude toward fasting. We learn from him why some fasting was unacceptable to God and what He desires instead.

Isaiah dealt with deep ethical questions in his prophecies to the nation of Israel. He represented the voice of God to a people with problems, to a nation whose spiritual comprehension left much to be desired.

God's concern is always with the heart. It is this that He examines when we approach Him with worship and service. When we fast, He asks us first of all, "What is your motive? What are you trying to accomplish with your fasting?"

As the Lord God examined the motives common in the Israel of Isaiah's day, He found self-righteousness clothed in externalism. People were substituting the machinery of fasting for true heart-engagement with the Lord. They were deceived regarding their own position of righteousness and were therefore unable to mourn for the condition of their hearts. Instead of humbling themselves, they made fasting an occasion for demanding results from God. In fact, they were complaining that God was not giving them the attention they deserved.

Their fasting was part of a religion of pretense. It exhibited the appearances of repentance while the heart was not being touched. These people did not see their need for change; they thought God was the one to change. They took fasting, the very means for repentance, and made it the occasion for further sin!

They sought to fool God with their outward manner, but in so doing they increased their self-deception. God could see through the hypocrisy, but they lost the knowledge of their own hearts. As their blindness grew, so did their belligerence. "What is the matter with God?" They had forgotten that prayer and fasting must begin with the question, "What is wrong with me? What do I need God to change within me?"

The nation seemed bewildered when Isaiah lifted his voice to show them their transgressions and sins. "Transgressions and sins? Indeed!"

"We seek the face of God daily and act as righteously as we are able. We have not forsaken the ordinance of God. In fact, it is quite the opposite. We delight in our service to God" (see Isaiah 58:2, 3).

They felt that the problem was not in them but in the Lord. They fasted, but God didn't notice it. They afflicted themselves, but He paid no attention. Why should condemnation be heaped upon them by the prophet? They were not to blame!

But God saw their entire attitude as sin. Is there any greater blindness than religious self-deception?

## God Requires Honesty

God's answer to the people's complaints abruptly called them back to reality. Fasting was to be born of obedience, not of self-will. It was to be initiated by God and done in His way. It was to manifest recognition of need for change. God could not consider what they were doing as fasting, even though the people did abstain from eating.

The reply of the Lord was, "Yes, you fast, but it is not a fast designed by Me. Your fasting is for strife, for debate, for personal pleasure, and to strike out at others. Your kind of fasting will not be accepted by Me" (see Isaiah 58:4).

Isaiah then proceeded to lay down the most comprehensive discourse on fasting recorded in the Bible.

He began with the issue of hypocrisy, the lack of conformity between outward actions and the condition of the heart. We are told that the Lord derives no pleasure in the outward mechanics of fasting if these are detached from inner reality.

> Is it such a fast that I have chosen? a day for a man to afflict his soul? is it to bow down his head as a bulrush, and to spread sackcloth and ashes under him? wilt thou call this a fast, and an acceptable day to the Lord?
>
> Isaiah 58:5

The general consensus seemed to have been, "Yes, this is precisely what we felt the Lord required of us. We understood that He wanted us to look sad, morose, and uncomfortable. Is this not the language for fasting? Is something more involved?"

## The Right Focus

Then the Lord began to deal with the matter of proper focus —focus away from themselves and what they were doing. Fasting was not only to set their focus upon God, but also upon the needs of others (see Isaiah 58:6-10). The shift of focus from ourselves to God enables us to receive a further shift in focus. God can specify how we are to look upon the needs of others, once He has our full attention. We cannot become involved with other people until we have been freed from self-preoccupation.

This is the area that makes fasting psychologically healthy and sound. It is the shifting of your attention and care from yourself to others. Religious focus can easily turn inward. Regrettably, this inward turn happens to many. This is especially true for those who inordinately desire to be used by the Lord. They reason, "Perhaps if I fasted, I could obtain more power, do more things, see more results, and be known by more people." This sounds good and extremely religious, but it is the wrong focus. The weight of attention is on what you will become.

Those who are psychologically healthy learn to become involved in the world outside themselves. Instinctively they reach out to care for others. They grow in involvement as they mature.

Fasting must deal with reality. We cannot skirt true issues. Fasting is not a means of escaping, but for fulfilling social responsibility. The fast God has chosen so prepares us within that we can be used to bring about change in outward circumstances. As we receive inner liberation, we in turn can bring deliverance and help to others.

But this release on the inside requires the penetration of truth. We must see ourselves as God sees us and then accept His mercy for what it is—unmerited favor freely extended to us. We are not receptive to God's mercy until we deeply and honestly acknowledge our need for change and our inability to accomplish this by ourselves. As we humble ourselves by allowing God to make us aware of our need and of His provision, His grace can flow to us and through us to others.

This was exactly what the fasters of Isaiah's day refused to do. They would not face life; they were not honest with themselves. Such a fast could not help anyone.

God put His finger on the ineffectiveness of their fasting by asking them to do precisely what they could not do—help others. Had they been fasting properly, involvement with others would have spontaneously resulted. But since their focus was introverted, they could not see the needs of others, let alone do anything about them. They had to see their shortcomings in a tangible way—by discovering their inability to obey. God in His mercy refused to allow them to continue in their self-deception. They could not go on hiding from themselves and from each other.

God has provided a gauge for genuine fasting. We can tell whether our fasting is acceptable to God by its results in our own lives and our effectiveness in relation to others around us. We need not be in the dark when we can check ourselves against His Word. If fasting is doing its work of liberating our focus from self-preoccupation, this will show in mercy toward everyone else. We will give what we are receiving from God.

The root of Israel's failure in fasting was self-centeredness. Their hearts were not focused upon God, for they had no knowledge of what God desired. Instead they were fasting with a focus on their own merits. Religion had become their own game and they were writing their own rules. They were even seeking to ignore life's built-in rules by withdrawing themselves from involvement with other people.

God has chosen a fast that is effective in self-denial and inner release. This fast cuts across self-will and causes us not only to focus upon God but to invest in others. God's chosen fast forces us to deal with the real world.

God's fast is motivated by a faith which works by love. It results not only in attitude change, but in action. Isaiah grouped these actions in two general categories: the first, of undoing; the second, of doing.

## The Undoing of Bondage

Isaiah 58 contains four verbs (*italics* added) which relate to deliverance or the undoing of harm and oppression:

> Is not this the fast that I have chosen? to *loose* the bands of wickedness, to *undo* the heavy burdens, and to *let* the oppressed go free, and that ye *break* every yoke?
>
> Isaiah 58:6

We are to untie the ties of habitual sin and then lift the crushing load of guilt, fear, and oppression. The oppressed can only be restored to normal liberty if he knows that his bondage to habit has been broken, that he will not be overpowered again. Guilt must be removed by the cleansing blood, fear banished by the knowledge of God's full acceptance, and heaviness replaced by freedom to praise God from the heart. Following the release of the oppressed, we must break every yoke that would again enslave him. The source of the temptation must be removed by imparting God's strength to the area which was weakened by repeated failure.

## The Sharing of Provision

Isaiah's second category of actions is that of positive contribution. We are not only to undo evil, but to do good. The four action-verbs (*italics* added) in verse seven all convey the idea of sharing.

> Is it not to *deal* thy bread to the hungry, and that thou *bring* the poor that are cast out to thy house? when thou seest the naked, that thou *cover* him; and that thou *hide not* thyself from thine own flesh?
>
> Isaiah 58:7

We are to break our own bread and share it with the needy. This is not some impersonal contribution to a welfare fund—good as this is—but taking some of our portion and personally distributing it among the needy. We are to bring the hungry to our home and set him at our table. When we see the need of clothing, food, or shelter, we are to share ours. This cannot be done without deep personal investment in the concerns of others. We must care to the extent that their need becomes our need, and our resources are unlocked because of compassion. The key to sharing is found in the last phrase, *and . . . hide not thyself from thine own flesh.*

The Hebrew word for *flesh* in this passage includes a broad scope of meaning: self, body, skin, and kin. The scriptural concept involves all these shades of meaning. We begin with self-awareness through honesty, but we go on to identify ourselves with all mankind and especially with our own flesh-and-blood relatives. Caring always begins with those immediately surrounding us, not with the millions across the sea.

Caring inevitably leads to sharing at the cost of inconvenience. Fasting attests our willingness for such sacrifice. The sacrifice God asks of us is to do good and share with those around us. The Hebrews' writer said:

But to do good and to communicate forget not: for with such sacrifices God is well pleased.

Hebrews 13:16

Paul said:

Distributing to the necessity of saints; given to hospitality.

Romans 12:13

Caring cannot stop with words, not even with religious words. Caring must be demonstrated. James asked:

If a brother or sister be naked, and destitute of daily food, And one of you say unto them, Depart in peace, be ye warmed and filled; notwithstanding ye give them not those things which are needful to the body; what doth it profit?

James 2:15, 16

The Apostle John gave us this test of genuineness:

Hereby perceive we the love of God, because he laid down his life for us: and we ought to lay down our lives for the brethren. But whoso hath this world's good and seeth his brother have need, and shutteth up his bowels of compassion from him, how dwelleth the love of God in him? My little children, let us not love in word, neither in tongue; but in deed and in truth.

1 John 3:16-18

Fasting prepares us for sacrificial giving because we first gain the discipline of self-denial. We get our minds off ourselves and reorder our priorities. We then become able to see our brother's need. Sharing is a spontaneous outflow of mercy when we have identified ourselves as on the same level as our brother. Humbling ourselves through fasting is a sure way to recognize how human we are.

## Fasting From Self-Service

A few years ago we saw this truth at a local church and consequently urged the people to fast from self-service. Instead of buying something for themselves, they were to buy for others. They were to purchase bread and meat for the hungry and give it away as they fasted. They were to do without extra clothes to clothe the naked. They were to fast from being oppressive and demanding. This meant that they were to stop being religious oracles who knew it all. They were not to pressure people, but to lift them. They must fast from doing "their own thing" and become involved with those around them who needed them—"their own flesh."

This is the way life is in the real world. If you seek your own, you eventually will have yourself on your own hands and in time you will become weary of yourself. Jesus warned us that if we try to save our lives, we will surely lose them. No man realizes his potential through self-service. Every successful person practices this part of God's chosen fast; he does so intuitively. The successful man gives himself away. The person who loses his life for others will find it.

No one in Isaiah's day seemed to have had the slightest notion that fasting involved this kind of ethical self-denial. They were sure that fasting was little more than an empty stomach and drab apparel. Too often we are guilty of thinking the same way.

## Showing Mercy

Isaiah added another area of abstinence to all of the above —fasting from judgment against others in any form. Only those who chose to show mercy would receive mercy. God would answer the cry of the person whose fast included the putting away of all self-righteousness and replacing it with genuine compassion.

> Then shalt thou call, and the Lord shall answer: thou shalt cry, and he shall say, Here I am. If thou take away from the midst of thee the yoke, the putting forth of the finger, and speaking vanity; And if thou draw out thy soul to the hungry, and satisfy the afflicted soul; then shall thy light rise in obscurity, and thy darkness be as the noon day.
>
> Isaiah 58:9, 10

Notice that God's promise is conditional. We cannot receive God's mercy until we have created capacity by showing mercy to others. We must eliminate the yokes, the critical finger, and speaking vanity. These three areas of abstinence are vital for each of us.

The *yokes* are unnecessary religious demands. The Pharisees at the time of Christ were accused of placing unbearable yokes upon men and then refusing to help in lifting them. This forced perpetual religious activity which prevented a man from ever arriving at a meeting with God. In contrast, the early Christians at the council of Jerusalem made a merciful decision concerning the Gentiles.

> Now therefore why tempt ye God, to put a yoke upon the neck of the disciples, which neither our fathers nor we were able to bear? But we believe that through the grace of the Lord Jesus Christ we shall be saved, even as they.
>
> Acts 15:10, 11

The pointing of the finger was a meaningful gesture among the Orientals. It was nonverbal language for contempt and scorn. Unfortunately, we say the same things in different ways today. We still criticize, accuse, and compare ourselves with others. Any expression of superiority is the same thing as *putting forth the finger*. Fasting is needed at this point.

A better translation of *speaking vanity* is "speaking wickedness." This includes every kind of insincerity, but especially refers to slander and gossip. The *Living Bible* renders it, "spreading vicious rumors."

Fasting, then, includes far more than abstinence from food; it involves ceasing from our own ways and serving others. It is indeed a focus of heart.

# Bibliography

Carter, Charles W., ed. *Wesleyan Bible Commentary.* Grand Rapids, Michigan: William B. Eerdmans Publishing Co., 1967, vol. I: p. 334.

Harrison, Everett F. et al., eds. *Baker's Dictionary of Theology.* Grand Rapids, Michigan: Baker Book House, 1969, p. 215.

Murray, Andrew. *With Christ in the School of Prayer.* Westwood, New Jersey: Fleming H. Revell Co., 1953, p. 74.

Lloyd-Jones, D. Martyn. *Studies in the Sermon on the Mount.* Grand Rapids, Michigan: William B. Eerdmans Publishing Co., 1960, vol. II: pp. 37, 38.

Prince, Derek. *Shaping History Through Prayer and Fasting.* Old Tappan, New Jersey: Fleming H. Revell Co., 1973.

Wallis, Arthur. *God's Chosen Fast.* Fort Washington, Pa.: Christian Literature Crusade, 1968, p. 16.